P9-AEX-512

U·N·I·Q·U·E·L·Y
SOUTH DAKOTA

Bob Karolevitz
and
Bernie Hunhoff

*This book is part of a
limited edition.*

NORWEST BANKS
SOUTH DAKOTA

Proud To Be With You.

This book is a look at the people who came before us. The people who through their hard work and sacrifices helped form the vibrant and exciting land called South Dakota. It is about the place we fondly call home…and it is about the many and varied treasures the entire country knows as South Dakota.

In celebration of 100 years of statehood, Norwest Bank South Dakota is privileged to bring you this limited edition of the South Dakota Pictorial History Book. We are proud to play a role in the continuing growth of this beautiful and progressive state. With this book, we renew our commitment to the people of our state and to future generations.

We are sure this outstanding work of history will be a treasured edition in your library for years to come.

C.P. Moore

C.P. Moore, Chairman

NORWEST BANKS
SOUTH DAKOTA

©1988 Norwest Bank South Dakota, N.A.   Equal Opportunity Lender   Member FDIC

South Dakota Tourism, Paul Horsted photo

U·N·I·Q·U·E·L·Y
SOUTH DAKOTA

by

Bob Karolevitz
and
Bernie Hunhoff

design by
Patrick S. Smith

THE
DONNING COMPANY
PUBLISHERS
NORFOLK/VIRGINIA BEACH

Copyright © 1988 by Robert (Bob) F. Karolevitz and
    Bernard (Bernie) Hunhoff, Jr.

All rights reserved, including the right to reproduce this work in
any form whatsoever without permission in writing from the
publisher, except for brief passages in connection with a review.
For information, write:

The Donning Company/Publishers
5659 Virginia Beach Boulevard
Norfolk, Virginia 23502

Edited by Amy E. M. Kouba
Richard A. Horwege, Senior Editor

Library of Congress Cataloging-in-Publication Data

Karolevitz, Robert F.
    Uniquely South Dakota.

    Bibliography: p.
    Includes index.
    1. South Dakota—History—Pictorial works. 2. South
Dakota—Description and travel—Views. I. Hunhoff, Bernie,
1951-   . II. Title.
F652.K37   1988   978.3   88-23743
ISBN 0-89865-730-X

Printed in the United States of America

South Dakota Tourism, Chad Coppess photo

CONTENTS

"The Harvest Orator" was painted by Harvey Dunn for the 1909 edition of "The Jack Rabbit," the yearbook of South Dakota Agricultural College. He received his first art training on the Brookings campus from Ada B. Caldwell, who, he said, opened new vistas for him. The painting recalled his own work days on his family's Kingsbury County homestead. South Dakota Art Museum

On November 2, 1889, President Benjamin Harrison was faced with the task of signing the proclamation that would create the "twin states" of North and South Dakota. It was one of those little quirks of history that a decision was made to carry out the legal action so that no one would ever know which of the two commonwealths was first to enter the Union.

Accordingly, the admission documents were shuffled under a covering paper so that the president couldn't see what he was signing. It was then that South Dakota became the 39th or 40th state. (Later, by common agreement and alphabetical order, North Dakota was accorded the earlier honor.)

It is the purpose of this book to commemorate—by camera's lens and artist's brush—that veiled signing and the first hundred years of the southernmost of the two mid-continental states.

This is *not* a definitive history! Instead it is a graphic view of a tenacious people on a unique portion of the world's globe. By necessity it has to be just a pictorial sampler of the people, places and events that together portray the growth and development of the state. Much more had to be left out than could be put in; the choices were the authors' prerogatives, for better or worse. The aim was to present the flavor of South Dakota and not the total substance.

Located as it is between the 43rd and 46th parallels, the state is the beneficiary (and sometimes victim) of a diversity of climate, which shapes its agricultural adaptability and provides its citizens

South Dakota's state flower, the purple pasque, is a harbinger of spring as it grows wild on river bluffs and unplowed pasture lands. South Dakota Tourism, Paul Horsted photo

with an invigorating four-season way of life. Within its 77,047 square miles is a wide range of geographical differences that further governs the social, economic and recreational activities of those who proudly claim kinship to the Land of Infinite Variety. From the undulating prairie of the east to the granite spires of the Black Hills in the west, there are dissimilar regions of glacial moraine, productive black loam, chalkrock river bluffs, shortgrass plains and the artistically eroded Badlands seemingly borrowed from the moon.

In prehistoric times, gargantuan dinosaurs, woolly mammoths, giant earth sloths and sabre-toothed tigers shared portions of an ever-changing terrain. They were joined or followed by lumbering rhinoceroses, tiny three-toed horses, four-pronged antelopes and over-sized predecessors of the later-day bison. Then, still clouded in the mysteries of the past, the first human inhabitants arrived.

Through the centuries these unknown South Dakotans were succeeded by Mound Builders and a passing parade of tribal people who—after the time of Columbus—came to be known as Indians.

In the late 15th century, European explorers preceded the eventual flow of colonizers in search of wealth, land and personal freedom. In time French voyageurs reached mid-continental America; and the historic visitation of Louis Joseph and Francois La Verendrye to the region that ultimately became South Dakota was attested to by the inscribed lead tablet they buried on the gumbo bluffs of the Missouri River in 1743.

The European concept of land ownership was applied to the new continent, and in 1803 President Thomas Jefferson acquired the vast interior expanse known as the Louisiana Purchase, which one day would encompass all or part of thirteen states, including the two Dakotas.

The creation of Dakota Territory in 1861 was the prelude to statehood for the plainsland to which eager settlers were lured by the cession of Indian lands, the Homestead Act, railroad expansion and the effusive promises of entrepreneurs and exploiters.

With this prologue to set the stage, the pages that follow present a pictorial view of two distinct sections that make up the 40th state: the east-river and west-river countries. These have been further divided into six less rigidly defined areas, based on a combination of geography and the progression of development. There are obvious overlappings, of course, but to tell the story graphically and with some semblance of organization, this format permits the most effective method of depicting the diversity involved.

In the end, when all the pieces are brought together, the final product is a kaleidoscopic portrait of a land and its people that can only be described as Uniquely South Dakota!

Perhaps nowhere in the world are sunsets, rainbows and massive cloud banks more picturesque than on the prairie. They are what artist Harvey Dunn called "the majesty of simple things." South Dakota Tourism

The Great Divider

The unpredictable Missouri River could be tranquil at times, raging at others. Poet John G. Neihardt referred to it as "the eternal Fighting Man" before it was somewhat tamed by the Pick-Sloan dams. Clyde Goin collection

South Dakota Tourism, Mark Kayser photo

To help one better understand South Dakota's unique split personality, it is logical to begin this extended pictorial essay by pointing out the role the Missouri River plays as it divides the state into two unlike sections almost equal in size.

In addition to geographical dissimilarities, the unusual dichotomy created by the Mighty Mo is reflected in various ways. South Dakotans—though they live in the same state—are often quick to identify themselves as being from "east river" or "west river." And, although the differences are mostly subtle, in such things as politics and economic pursuits, they sometimes can be quite obvious. A competitive spirit also exists because of the division.

For the Indians, the brown, sediment-laden river was both a blessing and an obstacle. Its shoreline provided willows, cottonwood and reeds for multiple uses; waterfowl, fish and small animal furs were an additional bounty from it. Because of treacherous eddies, its depth in some places and great width in others, the tribespeople did not travel back and forth across the *M'ME-sho-shay* as regularly as they did the more fordable streams.

While the Missouri was not used by the Sioux as a major artery of transportation, the river became the aquatic highway for the Lewis and Clark expedition on both the outbound and return trips. Explorers, fur traders and missionaries followed its meandering course, while trappers harvested rich hoards of beaver, mink, muskrat, marten and other furs from its thicketed banks and those of its numerous tributaries.

To Pierre Chouteau, Jr. goes the credit for introducing the steamboat to the upper Missouri in 1831, and from that time on the region would never again be the same. Smoke-spewing packet boats were able to bring in greater quantities of guns, steel traps, trading merchandise and (unfortunately) whiskey. On the downriver trips they were loaded to capacity with buffalo hides and bundles of pelts.

When the first military commanders came to the region, they recognized immediately the logistical value of the stream, as well as its tactical importance. Steamboats brought supplies to the forts and annuity goods to the Indian agencies. Then, when gold discoveries lured prospectors to Montana and Idaho, sternwheelers carried men and equipment upriver to Fort Benton and returned with their treasures of nuggets and dust.

Yankton and Fort Pierre were the principal ports of call in southern Dakota, giving them economic advantages not enjoyed by other new towns. However, they also attracted roustabouts, gamblers and the "soiled doves" of prostitution, who frequented the wharf areas. Operating the boats were men like Capt. Grant Marsh, who reputedly could navigate a shallow-draft vessel across "a sea of dew."

Romantic as it was, the steamboat era was relatively short-lived. The extension of railroad lines sounded the first death knell; and then a natural disaster—the destructive flood of 1881—battered and smashed the river fleet wintering in Yankton. With tonnage already seriously reduced by rail competition, the shipping industry never recovered.

For many years after that, the Missouri River was viewed more as a foe than as a friend. It chewed up valuable farm land with its capricious channel-changing habits, and the difficulties of crossing its relatively wide expanse limited trade and development. Ferry boats were slow and inconvenient, and pontoon bridges were sometimes treacherous and only temporary solutions. Winter permitted a few months of traffic—if the ice was thick enough. But by and large, the river was a hindrance to progress.

In 1907, railroad bridges were constructed at Pierre and the appropriately named new town of Mobridge, but it was 17 years before the first permanent highway span (a privately owned toll bridge) was festively opened for traffic at Yankton in 1924. Within the next two years, five publicly funded bridges were completed at Mobridge, Pierre, Chamberlain, Wheeler and Forest City.

Once the crossings were available, the next challenge was to harness and tame the mighty river to prevent floods, con-trol its voracious land-gobbling, provide irrigation and generate electricity. Prohibitive costs always sidetracked earlier ideas, but ironically—in the midst of World War II—Congress passed the Flood Control Act of 1944, which included the meshing of two separate proposals for the Missouri: one credited to Lt. Gen. Lewis A. Pick of the Corps of Engineers and the other to W. G. Sloan of the Bureau of Reclamation.

For South Dakota, the Pick-Sloan Plan became reality in the form of four major dams and the impoundments behind them: Gavins Point (Lewis and Clark Lake), Fort Randall (Lake Francis Case), Big Bend (Lake Sharpe) and Oahe (Lake Oahe). As a result, water-poor South Dakota became water rich! The mud-brown river turned misty green in some places and even deep-lake blue in others. Once a river of commerce and transportation, the Missouri had been altered into a giant recreational waterway. The state, previously renowned mostly for its pheasant hunting reputation, became equally famous for its catches of walleye, sauger, land-locked salmon and the strange, prehistoric paddlefish.

The Big Muddy—in the past always described as "too thick to drink and too thin to plow"—had evolved, with man's help, from threatening tyrant to faithful servant.

At Chamberlain, an ice jam on the Missouri destroyed part of the railroad bridge then under construction. To assist in replacing pilings, workmen inched a steaming locomotive onto a surviving section. By the summer of 1907, both the Milwaukee at Chamberlain and the Chicago and North Western at Pierre had spanned the river and had trains running to Rapid City. Chamberlain Register *collection*

The Missouri River steamboat fleet wintering at Yankton was battered to pieces by massive ice floes when the gorge broke in the destructive flood of 1881. The Western *was sunk and literally pulverized, while the* Butte *was broken in two. Other vessels severely damaged included the* Helena, *the* Black Hills, *the* Peninah, *the* Nellie Peck, *and the ferry* Livingston. W. H. Over Museum, Stanley J. Morrow collection*

Before railroad bridges were built across the Missouri at Chamberlain and Mobridge, rails were laid across the ice. It was a make-do situation at best, but it demonstrated the eagerness of the companies to extend their lines into the west-river country. E. S. Muxfelt collection

This mammoth catfish—an 85-pounder—was caught at the mouth of Choteau Creek, which separates Charles Mix and Bon Homme counties. The Missouri River and its tributaries produced numerous prize catches of this denizen of muddy waters, which gave variety to the diets of early pioneers. Douglas County Historical Society

South Dakota had no permanent road bridges across the Missouri River until 1924. Until then, crossings had to be made on the winter's ice, on pontoon bridges or using shallow-draft ferry boats. *The* Little Pearl, *left, ran between Running Water, South Dakota, and Niobrara, Nebraska, while the* Josie L. K. *served the Yankton area. Yankton County Historical Society*

The Forest City ferry was loaded to capacity with Indian children from the Cheyenne River Agency going on a picnic. South Dakota was fortunate that no major tragedies occurred when river crossings were dependent on rickety pontoon bridges and ferry boats not noted for safety features. *South Dakota State Historical Society*

Before the Missouri River was brought under control, its tributaries—like the Vermillion River in 1922—were subject to periodic and widespread flooding. The dams built after World War II did not completely eliminate the problem, but the odds against major disasters were greatly improved. *The University of South Dakota Alumni Association*

Artesian wells were a great boon to South Dakota farms and towns. Sometimes, though, they came in with such pressure that they were virtually uncontrollable. At Chamberlain, a well went wild and created this miniature Grand Canyon. *Siouxland Heritage Museums*

Promoters of the new Missouri River bridge at Chamberlain took an obvious swipe at the Yankton span with a "Free— No Toll" sign. By the late 1920s, highway bridges at Mobridge, Forest City, Pierre, Chamberlain and Wheeler provided west-river connections without charge, while tolls were not lifted from the Meridian Bridge at the Mother City until 1953. Chamberlain Register collection

Residents of Fort Pierre (right) and Pierre (below) were especially grateful for flood control dams on the Missouri River after both cities were inundated in 1952. Seasonal control of water levels and the alleviation of springtime ice gorges greatly reduced the dangers of such scenes being repeated. South Dakota State Historical Society

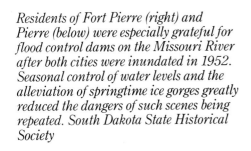

The ground-breaking for Gavins Point Dam near Yankton took place on May 18, 1952, with General Lewis A. Pick, Governor Sigurd Anderson of South Dakota and Governor Val Peterson of Nebraska officiating. Ironically, the dam was not built at Gavins Point as originally intended because a more feasible site was located farther downstream—but the name persisted. U.S. Army Corps of Engineers

South Dakotans once lived in a water-poor state where fishing, boating and swimming were limited forms of recreation in many areas. After the development of the giant reservoirs behind the dams on the Missouri, residents from border to border took to their man-made lakes almost as if they had always been there—and even flying water skiers were no longer an uncommon sight. U.S. Army Corps of Engineers

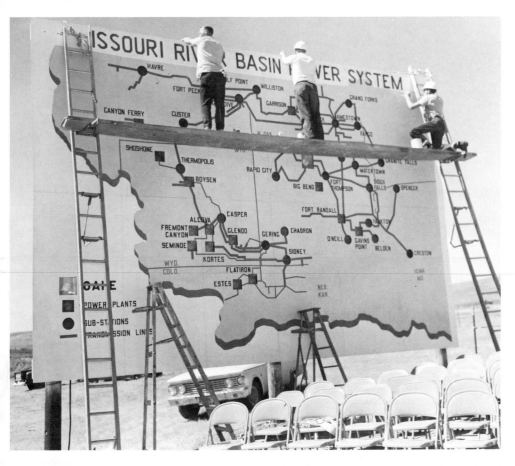

The widespread impact of the Missouri River dams was illustrated graphically by this giant display of the power system created. The exhibit was prepared for the visit of President John F. Kennedy for a dedication ceremony at the Oahe Dam in August of 1962. U.S. Army Corps of Engineers

Big Bend was the last of the six Pick-Sloan dams built on the Missouri River in the two Dakotas and Montana. It is located below the serpentine curve, which 18th-century explorers called the "Grand Detour." Near the site was the original location of Fort Thompson, an enclosed facility built in 1863 to incarcerate Santee and Winnebago Indians after the so-called Sioux Outbreak in Minnesota the previous year. The present-day town of Fort Thompson is located on the uplands adjacent to the dam. The reservoir was named for Governor M. Q. Sharpe of Kennebec, who seldom used his full name, Merrell Quentin. U.S. Army Corps of Engineers

Located just north of Pierre, Oahe Dam is one of the world's largest earth-fill river barriers, 9,300 feet long and 245 feet high. It was named for the old Oahe Indian Mission that was near the site. Oahe is a Sioux word meaning "foundation" or "a place to stand on." Lake Oahe is the longest of the Great Lakes of South Dakota, extending 231 miles upstream into North Dakota. It has a shoreline of more than 2,250 miles and is noted for walleye and salmon fishing. South Dakota Tourism

Six miles south of the town of Lake Andes, Fort Randall Dam began generating power in 1954, two years after closure was made to begin forming Lake Francis Case behind it. (Case, from Custer, served the state as a U.S. congressman and senator.) To provide living accommodations for construction workers, the government built Pickstown (in foreground), named for General Lewis A. Pick, co-author of the Pick-Sloan Plan and also the principal speaker at the ground-breaking ceremonies for this particular dam in 1946. U.S. Army Corps of Engineers

Gavins Point Dam, completed in 1957 near Yankton, is the farthest downstream of the Missouri River barriers within South Dakota. Besides its hydropower production, it is especially important to flood control in the southeastern corner of the state. By adjusting the level of the Missouri, it makes it possible for the James, Vermillion and Big Sioux Rivers to drain without obstruction. Lewis and Clark Lake behind the dam is the smallest of the so-called Great Lakes of South Dakota, but it has a shoreline of approximately 100 miles and an area of some 31,000 acres. Black Hills, Badlands & Lakes Association

The impoundments behind the Missouri River dams provide literally thousands of miles of lake shore which, in turn, offer endless opportunities to fish for everything from crappies to land-locked salmon, which were successfully planted in Lake Oahe. With its major attractions to outsiders previously limited mostly to pheasant hunting and the sights of the Black Hills and Badlands, South Dakota soon developed as a popular destination for diverse recreational activities after the dams were completed. U.S. Army Corps of Engineers

Ice fishing for northern pike, walleye and other species grew in popularity after the creation of the reservoirs behind the Missouri River dams. The introduction of powered augers, insulated clothing and various heating devices helped increase the number of enthusiasts for a sport previously enjoyed by only the hardiest winter anglers. South Dakota Tourism

A prize catch from the Missouri, the prehistoric paddlefish has a mouth big enough to gulp a loaf of bread but a throat so small that it can swallow only the tiniest plankton. It does not take bait but must be snagged with lead-weighted grappling hooks. With cartilage instead of bones, it has flesh similar to scallops and is a delicacy when properly prepared. Once erroneously labeled the spoonbill catfish, the odd creature can grow to well over 100 pounds. U.S. Army Corps of Engineers

Carp, buffalo and catfish were the principal catches of South Dakota anglers before the Great Lakes of the Missouri and improved stocking techniques began to develop the state's reputation for brag-worthy strings of sauger, walleye and land-locked salmon. These fishermen were obviously over-dressed for the sport. South Dakota Game, Fish and Parks Department

Representing the old and the new, a 20th-century Sioux Indian posed beside a portion of the Missouri River being tamed by the Oahe Dam construction project. The coming of the railroads, the discovery of gold in the Black Hills and the development of the Pick-Sloan Plan brought irreversible changes to the land and its people. U.S. Army Corps of Engineers

Yankton, known as the "Mother City of the Dakotas," grew from a mud-bound village to a prosperous small city because of its strategic location on the Missouri River. The *end of the steamboat trade and loss of the territorial capital to Bismarck in 1883 were temporary setbacks. Yankton County Historical Society*

The Historic Southeast

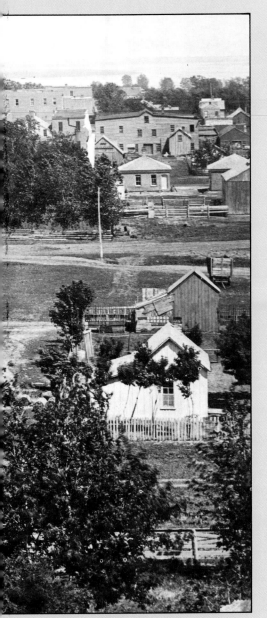

The mid-continental land that was to become South Dakota was officially opened to settlement in 1859 when the Yankton Indians ceded to the U.S. government some 14 million acres between the Missouri and the Big Sioux rivers.

A small band of opportunists waited on the Nebraska side of the Missouri for the dramatic departure of the Sioux from their camps along the river enroute to reservation confinement farther west. Almost before the dust settled behind the last travois, eager beneficiaries of that first cession treaty began staking their claims to portions of the mushrooming village of Yankton.

U.S. troops stationed upriver at Fort Randall had thwarted earlier attempts at settlement by "sooners" at Bon Homme, Elk Point and around Fort Vermillion. North along the Big Sioux, Indian raiders had chased off the founders of Medary and Flandreau; and at Sioux Falls City (which was founded in 1857 and abandoned five years later during the Santee Indian uprising), rival land companies unsuccessfully tried to establish a "squatter government."

When Dakota Territory was created in March of 1861, the mud-bound village of Yankton was designated as its capital. President Abraham Lincoln sent his family physician, William Jayne, to serve as the first governor of the sparsely populated, almost unmanageable frontier expanse, which encompassed all the future states of Montana, North Dakota, South Dakota and parts of Wyoming and Idaho.

To the disappointment of promoters, there was not a sudden rush of settlers into the region. The Civil War had curtailed railroad expansion, and disgruntled Indians—notably the Santees—added to the risk of homesteading. Gradually, though, the pace of immigration increased. The extension of the Dakota Southern Railroad from Sioux City to Yankton in 1873 was the harbinger of the Great Dakota Boom that followed.

Steamboat traffic on the Missouri, which flourished during the fur trade era, enjoyed a brief rejuvenation with the discovery of gold in the Black Hills. Meanwhile, the fertile farm land in the southeastern corner of the territory attracted increasing numbers of Scandinavians, Irish, Czechs, Dutch, Germans and other nationalities to the Dakota version of the American "melting pot."

They were the "Giants in the Earth" memorialized by novelist Ole Edvart Rolvaag, who immigrated to South Dakota, as did the fellow Norwegians he wrote about. They were the French Catholics in the vicinity of Jefferson who, in May of 1876, followed their pastor from field to field, praying and erecting the "grasshopper crosses." Legend says the prayer and crosses freed them from a devastating insect plague.

Included, too, were the Hutterian Brethren—German-speaking followers of the martyred Anabaptist, Jacob Hutter. They first arrived in the summer of 1874, not to take up homesteads, but to buy land so that they would not be obligated to the government for military service, which was against the tenets of their pacific religion.

Tiny towns sprang up along the rail lines, most with great expectations for the future. Not all of them made it, however. Almost lost in the cobwebs of history were such faded dreams as Blaha, Kingsburg, Perkins and Running Water in Bon Homme County; Lodi and Westerville in Clay; Spink and Nora in Union; Moe in Lincoln northwest of Hudson; and Janousek in Yankton.

Though it retained its historic title as "Mother City of the Dakotas," Yankton lost the territorial capital to Bismarck in 1883, two years after a disastrous ice-floe flood also brought to a boat-smashing end the river traffic so important to the town's economy. Meanwhile, a revived Sioux Falls had begun its accelerated growth, which eventually would make it the largest city in the state. In Vermillion, 35 students enrolled for the initial classes at the territorial university in 1882. Normal schools at Madison and Springfield, as well as the church-affiliated Yankton College, gave evidence of an early interest in education and cultural advantages.

Before statehood was achieved in 1889, the six-county area within and adjacent to the Sioux City-Yankton-Sioux Falls triangle was the seed-bed for eventual development elsewhere. When the seat of government was established in Pierre and an ever-expanding railroad network opened up the rest of the state for homesteading and town-platting, the southeast lost its gateway role and much of its earlier political influence.

Sioux Falls, on the other hand, continued to grow, becoming South Dakota's principal business, banking and transportation center—despite its location on the state's eastern periphery. Yankton, almost eight decades after its heyday as a rollicking river port, turned again to the Missouri as recreational areas at Gavins Point Dam began attracting visitors whose yearly numbers topped the state's total population.

Unfortunately, much of the physical evidence of the region's past—the territorial capitol, the steamboat landings and the protective stockades—did not survive the ravages of time or the demands for progress. But here and there, the undertones of history remain as silent reminders of a pioneer heritage.

Although the first train to cross the Minnesota border into Dakota was at Gary in 1871, the Dakota Southern Railway Company's extension from Sioux City to Yankton two years later was actually the first operating line within the future state. The "Judge Brookings," was the Dakota Southern's pride and joy, making the earliest run into the territory. Yankton County Historical Society

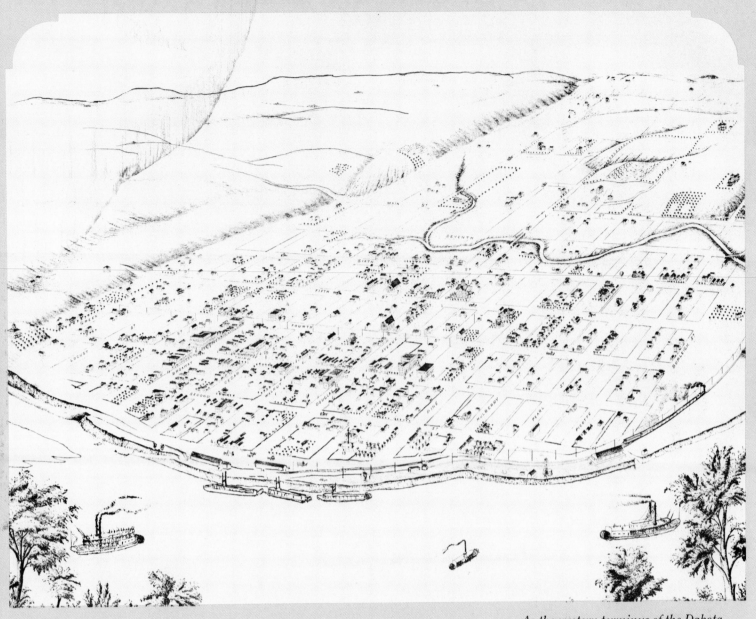

As the western terminus of the Dakota Southern Railway, Yankton—the territorial capital—was also a busy shipping port on the Missouri River during the 1870s and into the next decade. These steamboats were berthed at the foot of Douglas Avenue where artist Augustus Koch included three vessels in his 1875 drawing of the city. *W. H. Over Museum, Stanley J. Morrow collection (left), Yankton County Historical Society (above)*

South Dakota's first newspaper was The Dakota Democrat, *a "boomer" sheet that appeared at Sioux Falls City in July of 1859. It was published spasmodically until the editor departed for Missouri with the nameplate. It continued for a short while longer as the* Northwestern Independent. *South Dakota State Press Association*

Tyndall was named for John Tyndall, a British scientist who lectured throughout the United States before the town was founded in 1879. This vintage photograph of a Fourth of July celebration in the Bon Homme County seat was taken just before South Dakota became a state. Yankton County Historical Society

The flood of 1881 literally wiped out Vermillion's business district, which had been located on the lowlands below the Missouri River bluffs. It was then rebuilt on the high ground overlooking the broad valley. The Vermillion Standard was published in the building with the printing sign. W. H. Over Museum, Stanley J. Morrow collection

Frank Leslie's Illustrated Newspaper of April 16, 1881, carried a front-page drawing of the town of Vermillion in the flood of 1881. The disaster was the result of the river being backed up by ice gorges that finally gave way. South Dakota State Historical Society

In the early years especially, the Fourth of July was always a gala event, with parades, baseball games, fireworks and patriotic orators. In the 1880s, Sioux Falls (below) celebrated with a parade on Phillips Avenue, while in Yankton, spectators were treated to a lampooning of the Hunkpapa medicine man, Sitting Bull, then at the height of his notoriety and influence. Siouxland Heritage Museum, below; W. H. Over Museum, Stanley J. Morrow collection, right

The territorial legislature authorized a university at Vermillion in 1862, but it was 20 years before the first classes met under the direction of Dr. Ephraim Epstein, a former Jewish rabbi. In 1893 a fire gutted Old Main, the principal building, but the University of South Dakota quickly rebounded to become a widely respected institution of higher learning. At left is the historic structure as it was later restored. University of South Dakota

1874 ~ CENTENNIAL ~ 1974

Blizzard of 1888

In memory of these who
after wandering three miles
from school, were found
four days later
three miles due east of here.

FROZEN CHILDREN
JOHN ALBRECHT   JAN 12, 1888
PETER   GRABER   1875
HENRY KAUFMAN   1878
JOHN KAUFMAN   1877
ELIAS KAUFMAN   1874
                      1880

This is the earliest known picture of Armour, taken approximately two years before South Dakota became a state. In 1894 the busy railroad town replaced Grand View as the seat of government for Douglas County. Douglas County Historical Society

The tragic "children's blizzard" of 1888 struck on Thursday, January 12, as balmy weather of the morning changed suddenly to frigid temperatures and a heavy rain, which turned to sleet and then to granular snow. For more than a dozen hours the storm raged, catching farmers in the field and youngsters on the way home from school. On Friday the 13th survivors counted at least 112 dead in southern Dakota. Many more died later of complications from exposure, freezing and emergency amputations. This monument was erected in memory of five school boys who lost their lives near Freeman. Argus Leader

The nattily uniformed troopers of Company B stood for a final photograph at the Sioux Falls railroad station before departing for Washington, D.C., to participate in the inauguration ceremonies for President Benjamin Harrison on March 4, 1889. It was an exciting time because ten days earlier outgoing President Grover Cleveland had signed the Omnibus Bill, which paved the way for South Dakota's entry into the Union. President Harrison made it official on November 2 that same year. Siouxland Heritage Museums

The 1st South Dakota Volunteer Infantry Regiment was sent to the Philippines to battle insurrectionist troops during the Spanish-American War. All but two days of the action occurred after the U.S. Senate had ratified a peace treaty with Spain. Disease took a greater toll than bullets, and there was much grumbling at home about the boys being stuck in the jungles and rice paddies, still fighting when the war was over. Company C of the South Dakota Guards, in formation at Yankton in 1898, was one of the units involved. Yankton County Historical Society

In 1903 Theodore Roosevelt spoke from a flag-bedecked platform at Third and Walnut streets in Yankton. It took a booming voice for politicians and other orators to be heard by milling crowds in the days before public address systems. Yankton County Historical Society

Yankton was one of four registration points for the first Rosebud Reservation opening in 1904. Altogether, 106,296 hopeful homesteaders and speculators participated in the lottery, 57,494 of whom signed up in Yankton. Only 2,412 claims were awarded in the drawing. Richard V. Johnson collection

Coaling towers and turn-tables were important facilities during the steam era of railroading in South Dakota. Yankton, where these pictures were taken, was once served by the Milwaukee, Great Northern and Chicago and North Western lines. E. S. Muxfelt collection, left; Yankton County Historical Society, below

The local depot—like the Great Northern station at Yankton (right)—was the small town's connecting link to the outside world. The daily trains picked up and delivered mail, newspapers, cream cans, passengers, merchandise of all kinds and occasionally a coffin of a dearly departed. At Delmont in Douglas County (below) the dray wagons of Dan Teske and Henry Anderst provided the next step in the transport system. E. S. Muxfelt collection

As permanent settlements developed, flour mills were erected where streams could be dammed to provide the necessary water power. The mill at left was located on the Vermillion River six miles south of Centerville in Clay County. At Yankton on a Missouri River bluff, the Fountain Roller Mills facility (below) depended on what promoters thought would be unending artesian power. Unfortunately, indiscriminate drilling eventually reduced the pressure on all of the city's wells. South Dakota State Historical Society, left; Yankton County Historical Society, below

White's Mill on the James River near Mitchell provided flour-grinding facilities for area homesteaders before it was finally abandoned. Undependable water supply and overly optimistic projections of future populations contributed to the demise of various milling operations. Friends of the Middle Border Museum

Most small towns had at least one hotel or a boarding house, especially if they were located on a railroad line. In Armour—named for Philip D. Armour, a Chicago meat-packing tycoon—Boylan's Hotel (above) and the Armour House (its lobby shown at left) accommodated visiting drummers, as salesmen were known in those days. Douglas County Historical Society

The Cascade Milling Company in Sioux Falls was built in 1878. Powered by the waters of the Big Sioux River, it produced flour until after the turn of the century. Even more important was the generating plant that was erected next to this wooden structure in 1887. It served the city's electricity needs until 1901. Siouxland Heritage Museums

Tiny towns, usually the products of railroad extensions, faced the future with optimism in their early years. In the Yankton County town of Volin, boosters took their auto caravan on the road to promote business and real estate. Later, when the trains no longer came, many aspiring metropolises lost their schools, banks and occasionally their post offices as populations shifted to larger cities. Yankton County Historical Society

The 1911 Fourth of July parade in Corsica gave strong indication that the days of the horse and buggy were about over. It was a special year for celebrations because it marked the 50th anniversary of the creation of Dakota Territory. Douglas County Historical Society

In the summer of 1911 the 50th anniversary of the establishment of Dakota Territory was celebrated in Yankton, the former territorial capital. One of the returnees for the "Home Coming" event was Dr. William Jayne, who was the first governor. This photo was taken looking west on Third Street from the corner of Douglas Avenue. Yankton County Historical Society

The James River—known locally as the "Jim"—stretches across the entire state from north to south. Because of the minimal drop in elevation along its course, it is one of the slowest flowing rivers on the continent. Its annual "June rise" brought regular lowland inundations and occasional extensive floods such as this one in 1916. Yankton County Historical Society

Every town had its livery barn, while stables and carriage houses were built in the alleys behind many private homes. For at least two decades, horses and motor cars shared the streets and roads until the automobile finally took over. *Wall Drug Store collection, right; Center for Western Studies, below*

In 1890 the South Dakota Rapid Transit and Railroad Company introduced the state's first electric trolleys in Sioux Falls. The Sioux Falls Traction Company operated a fleet of cars on five lines before the system was discontinued in 1929. *Center for Western Studies*

Firefighting was a critical matter in small towns where wood construction was predominant. Competitions between fire departments had both a practical and sporting side. This team at Parkston in 1914 showed the intensity of a race against time. *South Dakota State Historical Society*

The state's history includes numerous political battles over the location of county seats. Reminiscent of one was the old deserted courthouse at Wheeler in Charles Mix County, which lost the government honors to Lake Andes. The reservoir behind Fort Randall Dam later inundated the site of the historic river town. *South Dakota State Historical Society*

Tom Shaw, the popcorn and peanut man, had a magnetic attraction for youngsters in the town of Armour. It was an era of unsophisticated entertainment: of parades, street carnivals and baseball games at the town park. Douglas County Historical Society

The town band was almost as important as the town baseball team when there was no radio or television for entertainment. In the earlier years, most bands—like this one in Freeman—were typically all-male groups. Pine Hill Printery

Women joined the men in this hunting party near Milltown on the James River in Hutchinson County. The Chinese ringneck pheasant, which came to South Dakota by way of Oregon, thrived and multiplied rapidly in the state, which authorized its first open season in 1919. Douglas County Historical Society

Bass Beach was one of the most popular resorts in southeastern South Dakota before and after World War I. Dances and celebrations of all kinds were held at the pavilion at Lake Andes. The 6,400-acre natural lake in Charles Mix County was also a favorite camping spot in the early days of automobile touring. Douglas County Historical Society

Pupils at the Lutheran Normal School in Sioux Falls were lined up for a spell-down or some other class exercise. Parochial schools operated by Dutch Reformed, Mennonite, Catholic and other religious denominations supplemented the public educational system throughout the state's first century, although rising costs and declining enrollments caused many of them to close after World War II. South Dakota State Historical Society

After World War I, surplus equipment was made available for road building throughout the United States. South Dakota benefited from the dispersal of military trucks and heavy construction vehicles, but the horse continued to be an important factor for at least another decade. Yankton County Historical Society

The first permanent bridge across the Missouri in South Dakota was built at Yankton in 1924. It had a lift span to permit vessels like the Douglas to pass beneath. The bridge was financed with private capital, and tolls were charged until 1953. Earlier crossings had to be made by pontoon bridges, which were subject to the whims of the weather and the sometimes treacherous currents of the river. Yankton County Historical Society, above; Robert E. Kolbe collection, left

The Gurney Seed & Nursery Company has been a nationally known South Dakota institution since it was moved to Yankton from Nebraska in 1894. The firm's main building (pictured above in the early 1930s) housed a variety of enterprises, including radio station WNAX, known in its early years as "The Voice of the House of Gurney." Always promotion conscious, the Gurneys took advantage of every opportunity to entertain visitors, including elephant rides, free pancake feeds, amateur contents and other customer-pleasing gimmickry. Yankton County Historical Society

Lawrence Welk, the farm boy from Strasburg, North Dakota (with accordion), got his start to national television fame on Yankton's pioneer radio station, WNAX, during the late 1920s. Before his popular Champagne Music was created, he led musical groups with names like the Hotsy Totsy Boys and the Honolulu Fruit Gum Orchestra. South Dakota State Historical Society

The Gurney peony farm on the outskirts of Yankton was the colorful scene of an annual gathering of flower lovers. A 1924 wedding held amid the perfumed air of the grounds was a special attraction. Standing behind the bride and groom was D. B. Gurney, one of nine sons of Colonel C. W. Gurney, the founder of the company who died in 1913. South Dakota Magazine

48

Communal living Hutterites (often mistak-enly called Mennonites) have been part of the South Dakota scene since the first three colonies were established in the 1870s. The Bon Homme, Wolf Creek and Old Elm Springs bands—numbering less than 400 in all—grew and prospered, though their apparel remained relatively unchanged for generations as they preserved the German language and the tenets of their religious faith. Traditionally camera-shy, colony children posed for this picture. Clyde Goin collection

When the automobile replaced Old Dobbin, the business sections of South Dakota towns took on a new look. By the late 1920s and early '30s, cars were commonplace, and livery stables and hitching posts disap-peared. Pictured here are the Main Streets of Marion (right) and Yankton (below). Note in the latter photo that a room in the Coates Hotel was available for 50 cents a night. South Dakota State Historical Society

President Theodore Roosevelt greeted well-wishers in Sioux Falls from the back seat of a Fawick Flyer, manufactured locally by Thomas O. Fawick, who had started building motor cars as a teenager. It was advertised as America's first four-door automobile, but, for better or worse, Sioux Falls did not become a second Detroit. *South Dakota State Historical Society*

At the Sioux Falls Air Base in 1944, women of the city prepared a festive Seder meal for Jewish servicemen on the eve of Passover. It was just one of many activities that evidenced South Dakota's all-out support of the nation's war effort. *Center for Western Studies*

The first school house in Dakota Territory—at the village of Bon Homme, which no longer exists—was commemorated by a parade float in the annual Czech Days celebration at Tabor (left). A monument and replica of the school is at the original site in southern Bon Homme County (below left). The first permanent school house in the territory—erected at Vermillion 1864—is also appropriately remembered (below right). Yankton County Historical Society, *left and below right;* South Dakota Magazine, *below left*

51

A demonstration of pioneer grain-
harvesting techniques was a feature of
Czech Days at Tabor in 1958. Czechs—or
Bohemians, as they are often called—
settled extensively in Charles Mix, Bon
Homme and Yankton counties. Yankton
County Historical Society

As railroads served earlier generations, South Dakota's two interstate highways provided sorely needed transportation arteries. This portion of the north-south

Interstate 29 on the eastern fringe of the state, near Beresford, was dedicated on September 30, 1962, by Governor Archie Gubbrud (front center in light coat).

Interstate 29 intersects with the east-west Interstate 90 at Sioux Falls. South Dakota State Historical Society

South Dakota is an agriculturally dependent state, so lush fields of small grain are vital to a healthy economy. Corn, soybeans, alfalfa and sunflowers are other major crops grown principally in the east-river country. South Dakota State University

Land of the Glaciers

At some period clothed in the mysteries of geological time, vast sheets of ice edged down from the north onto the land destined to become South Dakota. The northeastern portion of the future state was especially affected as the glaciers relentlessly bulldozed their way southward, piling up earthen debris in some areas and gouging out lake beds and potholes in others.

This phenomenon of the Pleistocene Epoch created the Coteau des Prairie, the broad, fertile valley of the James River and the smaller troughs of other lesser streams. Before the ebbing began, the western extremities of the ice masses formed the original channel of the Missouri. Thereafter, the unfettered river shaped and reshaped to its own whimsical designs.

Aeons later, the mysterious Mound Builders left their traces along the Big Sioux River and in the vicinity of Big Stone Lake. They were followed in time by nomadic tribes in pursuit of bison herds on one hand and pressured westward by better armed Indian enemies on the other. Apparently the first Europeans to reach the coteau region of South Dakota were French fur traders employed by Daniel Greysolon, the Sieur Dulhut (Duluth), who crossed the then-undefined Minnesota border in the summer of 1679.

It was more than a century and a half later before Lt. John C. Fremont, the Great Pathfinder, surveyed the lake region and left his mark through the names he ascribed to the various bodies of water he identified and plotted on his maps. Lake Benton he named for his future father-in-law, Senator Thomas Hart Benton of Missouri; Lake Preston for Senator William Campbell Preston of South Carolina; and Lake Poinsett for Joel Roberts Poinsett, the secretary of war whose memory has been further perpetuated in the poinsettia, the Christmas flower he introduced to the United States from Mexico.

A few French traders and trappers took up temporary residence west of Lake Traverse and Big Stone Lake in the pre-settlement era. And in 1864, Fort Wadsworth (renamed Fort Sisseton three years later) was established to protect non-belligerent Wahpeton and Sisseton Indians from the hostile Santees. In 1867 the odd triangle-shaped Lake Traverse Reservation was created by treaty for the Wahpetons and Sissetons.

As they had been elsewhere, railroads and the Homestead Act were the catalysts for settlement in the region. Intense rivalry between the Chicago and North Western and the Chicago, Milwaukee and St. Paul companies spurred an influx of farm-seekers and town-developers in the late 1870s and early 1880s. The Dakota Central division of the C. and N. W. extended its trackage from Tracy, Minn., to Brookings, then on to Huron and Pierre, creating other hopeful towns along the way. The extension of its Winona and St. Peter division from Gary to Lake Kampeska and beyond brought the excitement of the Great Dakota Boom to Watertown, Redfield and smaller communities in between.

Farther north the C. M. & St. P. (known popularly as the Milwaukee Road) crossed the border at Big Stone City and moved westward to Milbank in 1880. After that the towns of Webster, Bristol, Andover and Groton sprang up along the extended line, which eventually reached Aberdeen in the summer of 1881. In the haste to attract homesteaders, sometimes ties and rails were hurriedly laid atop virgin sod with the intention of constructing a better roadbed later. It was a rule of thumb for the railroad companies to establish sidings between seven and ten miles apart, the concept being to make it possible for most farmers to get to a rail stop by horse and wagon and back home again during the same day.

As north-south connecting lines were constructed, the railroads tied together the dozens of villages whose citizens generally had visions of grandeur for the future. Unfortunately, not many of the dreams were realized; and a century later, when tracks and depots disappeared, so did schools and post offices in some of the once eagerly expectant communities.

Aberdeen, strategically situated where railroads and highways crossed, became a hub city for commerce and warehousing, as did Watertown farther east. In 1883 the territorial legislature appropriated $25,000 to establish the Dakota Agricultural College (which evolved into

South Dakota State University) at Brookings. An unusual outcropping of granite in Grant County provided Milbank with its own unique quarrying industry.

Literally millions of waterfowl use the lakes formed by glacial action as stopover points or for nesting areas, but the region's most unusual geographical feature is the north-south continental divide between Lake Traverse and Big Stone Lake. Outlet waters from Lake Traverse flow northward to drain into Hudson Bay through the Red River of the North; those from Big Stone Lake eventually make their way to the Mississippi. Strangely enough, many South Dakotans are unaware of this topographical quirk of nature, which has been called one of the best kept secrets in the state.

Farther south in Kingsbury County is De Smet, the "Little Town on the Prairie" made famous in the novels of Laura Ingalls Wilder. Readers and television viewers of all ages make pilgrimages to the scene of the homesteading experiences they have shared vicariously with the author. In the process, they have come to know better the uniqueness of the "land of the glaciers," where many hundreds of other families like the Wilders faced the same challenges in unremembered anonymity.

Waubay—an English corruption of a Sioux word meaning "where wild fowl build their nests"—was first called Station 50 when the Milwaukee Road arrived in 1880. For several years it was also known as Blue Lakes. A product of the Great Dakota Boom, the Day County town once had eleven grain elevators in operation. South Dakota State Historical Society

Like most South Dakota towns, Ashton in Spink County owes its early life to the railroad. The Chicago, Milwaukee and St. Paul line came through in 1881, missing an earlier settlement on the James River several miles south. The relocated town was called New Ashton for a time. South Dakota State Historical Society

56

Wherever the railroads went, grain elevators mushroomed up along the tracks to
handle the produce of the prairie. Farmers
hauled their grain to towns like Webster
and went home with wagon loads of flour,
livestock feed, coal and other supplies.
South Dakota State Historical Society

While the Milwaukee and North Western
companies dominated the early decades of
railroading in South Dakota, the Minneapolis and St. Louis line was extended into
Watertown in 1884 and later moved westward to Conde, Aberdeen and Le Beau.
The "Louie," as it was known, transported
thousands of cattle out of Le Beau when it
was in its heyday, and in 1906 it moved
carloads of water from Lake Kampeska to
Aberdeen when the Hub City suffered a
severe shortage. Jokingly referred to as the
"Miserable & Still Limping," the "Musty
& Stale" and other uncomplimentary
appellations, the Minneapolis and St. Louis
finally ceased operations in 1960. *Codington County Historical Society*

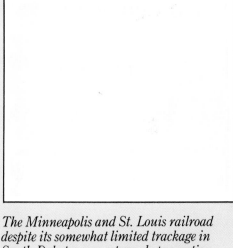

The Minneapolis and St. Louis railroad
despite its somewhat limited trackage in
South Dakota, was extremely promotion
conscious in its efforts to develop business.
It advertised Indian land homesteads, Lake
Kampeska excursions and special trains to
baseball and football games in Minnesota.
South Dakota State Historical Society

The arrival of the first highly publicized
Olympian train in Milbank was an occasion for celebration. The Grant County
town was named for a director of the Milwaukee Road, Jeremiah Milbank. *Grant
County Review collection*

Soddies, made of virgin prairie grass "bricks," provided the first housing for numerous South Dakota pioneers. The crude structures were reasonably cool in summer and warm in harsh winters, but there was a darkness and dankness about them that coats of whitewash and newspaper wall coverings could not completely offset. Wall Drug Store collection

Breaking up the tough prairie sod was a challenge for man, beast and machine. Pioneers used oxen and crude equipment. The introduction of huge steam tractors started the evolution from small farm operations to huge acreages of grain. The steam behemoths required an ever-present water wagon. Wall Drug Store collection, below; South Dakota State Historical Society, left

The nomadic frontier photographer Stanley J. Morrow had a lean-to studio while he was at Fort Wadsworth (later renamed Fort Sisseton). A native of Ohio, Morrow had been a photographer in the Union Army during the Civil War, moving to Dakota Territory in 1868. His wife, Isa, accompanied him on a number of his photographic missions. W. H. Over Museum, Stanley J. Morrow collection

Long before the days of radio and television, South Dakotans had to create their own home entertainment. In Bryant, the Charles Ahsmus family demonstrated a variety of diversions available, including music, reading, needlework, dramatics, miniature trains and stereopticon slides. Codington County Historical Society

What jazz combos and rock bands were to later generations, The Three Graces were to appreciative audiences in the 1880s. They performed in Madison and other southern Dakota communities in the days of minstrels, orators and lantern-slide presentations. Friends of the Middle Border Museum

In the years following statehood, the Chatauqua movement spread from border to border as South Dakotans hungered for cultural fare. Most towns erected tents for such performances, but at Lake Madison, a grand hotel and resort were built in 1891.

The resort included an auditorium that seated 2,500. As many as five passenger trains arrived daily during the Chatauqua summer, delivering visitors eager "for an intellectual feast." Robert E. Kolbe collection

When Oliver and Mary Bowman established the Montrose Herald in 1886, they commissioned artist Amasa James Arnold to engrave a nameplate for their new paper.

The classic design was still being used a century later as it depicted pioneering days in the Vermillion River valley. South Dakota Press Association

Patriotism ran high among citizens of the new state of South Dakota, and veterans of the Civil War were especially prominent in parades and civic celebrations. In Watertown in 1898 members of the Freeman-Thayer Post of the Grand Army of the Republic posed in front of their meeting hall (left), while at Hurley in Turner County, the E. S. McCook Post of the G.A.R. erected an inspiring memorial. Codington County Historical Society, left; South Dakota State Historical Society, below

Farming practices in South Dakota and throughout mid-America were revolutionized because of the research of Dr. Niels E. Hansen (right), a Danish immigrant who became a professor of horticulture at South Dakota Agricultural College in 1895. His introduction of a hardy strain of alfalfa from Siberia generated an important forage industry in the state, with especially heavy production concentrated in the vicinity of Gayville, which local residents like to call the "Hay Capital of the World." South Dakota State University, right; Missouri Valley Observer, above

October 1, 1896, was a red-letter day for South Dakota farmers and ranchers. That's when Rural Free Delivery service was established. It was a luxury for isolated homesteaders miles from the nearest post office. Robert E. Kolbe collection

Aberdeen in the early 1900s gave evidence of its eventual role as the Hub City in the northern tier of east-river counties. It was founded in 1881 and named for Aberdeen, Scotland, the native city of Alexander Mitchell, then general manager of the Chicago, Milwaukee and St. Paul Railroad. Authors Hamlin Garland and L. Frank Baum (who wrote The Wizard of Oz*) were among its early residents. Center for Western Studies*

Some of the smallest towns in the state built grand school houses as a show of faith in the future. At Pierpont in Day County, this classic structure was erected in 1904 when the town was 21 years old. Robert E. Kolbe collection

Though taken a generation or more apart, these pictures of White in Brookings County (above) and White Rock in Roberts County (right) revealed the sameness of small town Main Streets. In the far northeastern corner of the state, White Rock is on the Red River near its emergence from Lake Traverse. South Dakota State Historical Society

A city was well on the road to sophistication when its principal street was finally paved. It happened in Watertown in about 1910. The process was slow and involved lots of shovels, wheelbarrows and human muscles. Codington County Historical Society

Horses, a steam tractor and new-fangled gas-driven automobiles represented the progression of power sources on the farm (right). While the operation seems crude by later-day standards, an imagintive farmer rigged up his threshing machine so the straw would go directly into his barn (below), while a hose from an artesian well kept his water wagon supplied without constant hauling. South Dakota State Historical Society

Corn-picking contests drew huge crowds in the days before mechanical harvesting replaced the hand operation. This well-attended event took place near the village of Kampeska west of Watertown. Expert pickers required a combination of athletic skill, keen eyesight, coordination and stamina. Codington County Historical Society

Bert Waldo used this International Harvester high-wheeler for stocking fish in Lake Traverse. Small fry were transported in cream cans in the early efforts to develop the state's fisheries. South Dakota Game, Fish and Parks Department

As it did elsewhere, the automobile came to South Dakota during the first decade of the twentieth century, and the transition from horse to motorized transportation had begun. This was the Martin Geving blacksmith shop and garage at Nunda in Lake County. *South Dakota State Historical Society*

6542-S
D

Milbank, known for its granite quarries, engaged in a heated battle with Big Stone City before it eventually became the Grant County seat of government. In the early days of the auto era, the town was proud of its concrete sidewalks and street lights. Grant County Review *collection*

Troops departing for service in World War I brought crowds to the railroad stations at Redfield (above) and other South Dakota towns. The patriotic fervor was to be repeated a generation later—but after that the public attitude toward going to war changed. South Dakota State National Guard Museum, above; Yankton County Historical Society, right

South Dakota History, *the State Historical Society's quarterly magazine, illustrated the progression of wash day on the farm with these graphic photos. The tub-and-washboard drudgery (above) was sucseeded by the luxury of machines with the coming of the Rural Electrification Administration in 1935. Preceding the REA by a dozen years was an experimental 8½-mile rural electric line near Renner built by the Northern States Power Company. It served just 17 families. South Dakota State Historical Society*

Milbank in Grant County was the founding site of American Legion baseball. Since 1925, when the idea was conceived, scores of major leaguers have begun their careers as graduates of this nationwide program for teenagers. South Dakota State Historical Society

Uniforms weren't always easy to come by and equipment was minimal, but the smallest towns—and even crossroads communities—had their baseball teams. Commemo- *rating the history of the national sport in South Dakota, a baseball hall of fame and museum were established at Lake Norden. Frank B. Karolevitz Family collection*

The Black Blizzards of the Dirty Thirties were the direct result of drouth—but, admittedly, excessive cultivation of the prairie and poor conservation practices added to the severity of the storms. Street lights were required in mid-afternoon in *Watertown (above), as they were elsewhere throughout the state, and the silty dust drifted like snow along the rural fence lines. Codington County Historical Society, above; Wall Drug Store collection, below*

In addition to the drouth and economic depression, the Dirty Thirties brought a plague of grasshoppers to South Dakota. They demolished grainfields, ate paint off of buildings and were so thick on railroad tracks that they caused locomotive drive wheels to spin. The pile of dead insects (right) was raked off a small plot after a single poisoning. *South Dakota State Historical Society*

These proud anglers posed with their string of 102 fish, which they caught in one of the glacial lakes in less than two hours. Codington County Historical Society

The northeastern glacial region has provided a continuing harvest of waterfowl for both local and visiting hunters since pioneering days. In 1898 the sloughs around Arlington offered good duck shooting for this nondescript party of nimrods (right). Four years later, five hunters (below) near Watertown averaged almost a goose a minute in a 35-minute shotgun barrage. South Dakota State Historical Society, right; Codington County Historical Society, below

The Dakota Central Telephone Company brought phone service to Watertown, and the words "Hello, Central" soon became a part of the language of subscribers. Switchboards like these appeared throughout the state, as rural phone lines were erected with crude equipment and hand labor. Codington County Historical Society, _____; center for Western Studies, _____

Before World War II, South Dakota State College (later University) was known as the "West Point of the Prairies" because of the extent of its Reserve Officers Training Corps (ROTC) program. Military parades on the Brookings campus were impressive events. General Omar Bradley was once the ranking professor of military science and tactics at the school. South Dakota State University

At times, troop trains brought more than 500 soldiers a day through Aberdeen during World War II. And it was a stop the young servicemen remembered. Along with the standard luncheon fare served at the Aberdeen Canteen, a patriotic crew of Red Cross volunteers offered chopped pheasant sandwiches. Special hunts were conducted at towns throughout the region to supply the birds. By the war's end, more than half a million soldiers were served. South Dakota Game, Fish and Parks Department

One of the nation's most unique football homecomings is Hobo Day at South Dakota University. It had its beginning in 1912 when men students dressed like "knights of the road" and women like Indian maidens to march to the Brookings railroad station to greet the visiting team from Yankton College. The idea caught on, and a tradition developed. For many years the students "bummed" food on that day from local housewives, while the Hobo Day parade became one of the state's annual highlights. The 1912 celebrants gathered on the campus for this vintage photo. South Dakota State University Alumni Association

Centerpiece of South Dakota State University's Hobo Day celebration is its most revered relic, a 1912 Model T Ford known as the Bummobile. Numerous state and national celebrities have ridden in the historic auto, including presidential candidate Dwight D. Eisenhower, then on a campaign visit to Brookings in 1952. South Dakota State University

In the 1930s, South Dakotans participated in numerous recreational activities to take their minds off of drouth and depression. Softball games, marble tournaments and even ping pong matches were among the various events, some of which were sponsored by New Deal programs. In Milbank, a log-sawing competition drew a large crowd. Grant County Review *collection*

Fort Sisseton in Marshall County was originally established in 1864 as Fort Wadsworth, following the uprising of Santee Indians in Minnesota two years earlier. It was renamed in 1876 for the tribe that had settled in the area. The post's officers' quarters, barracks, powder magazine and guard house have been restored, and in the summer, visitors can watch a reenactment of an artillery squad in gun drills. *South Dakota Tourism*

Granite quarries in and around Milbank produce distinctive rose and purple-hued memorials and building stones for a worldwide market. The immensity of one of the Dakota Granite Company quarries can be appreciated by the comparative size of the worker on a stone in the lower center of the picture (below). The company's power plant and compressor room are on the edge of the quarry. Grant County *Review collection*

Horses, hayracks and hand-pitched bundles are reminders of earlier agricultural practices. Nostalgic yearning for "the old ways" has generated a keen interest in restoring steam engines and other farm equipment of past generations. They are demonstrated by willing workers at fairs, community anniversaries and such popular attractions as the Prairie Village near Madison. South Dakota State University, left; Joel Strasser photo, below

In 1898 students at the South Dakota Agricultural College in Brookings learned about the latest technological developments on the farm. Mammoth steam tractors were replacing horses and oxen where practical, and mechanical training became an important part of the curriculum of the land-grant college. South Dakota State University

Author Hamlin Garland, who homesteaded briefly in northeastern South Dakota during the 1880s, wrote of enormous flocks of ducks and geese that settled on the fields "like some prodigious cataract from the sky." Located on a major migratory route, South Dakota continues to attract massive flights of waterfowl. At the Sand Lake National Wildlife Refuge north of Columbia, more than a quarter of a million snow geese are annual visitors. The Waubay National Wildlife Refuge in Day County lives up to the Sioux definition of Waubay as "a nesting place for birds." South Dakota Tourism, Paul Horsted photo

The Big Stone Power Plant, which began operations in Grant County in 1975, provides 415,000 coal-produced kilowatts of electricity for nearly a million users in South Dakota and surrounding states. It requires an average of 80 100-ton rail cars of North Dakota lignite daily—an annual total of more than two million tons. South Dakota Tourism

The Panoramic Prairie

When the first white settlers came to southern Dakota, they found an expansive rolling grassland, mostly devoid of trees and still showing evidence of the immense herds of bison that once had roamed unhampered across the fenceless plains.

Through the years, plow and harrow broke much of the virgin sod, while farmsteads and tiny towns sprang up along crisscrossing railroad lines. Though shelterbelts, silos and water towers eventually disturbed the uncluttered horizon, the French word "prairie" continued to be appropriately descriptive of the undulating terrain between South Dakota's rivers.

This was the "elbow room" cherished by hardy homesteaders, a land of unique beauty punctuated in the spring and summer seasons by the purple pasque and other native flowers. There was also a harsh reality to test the mettle of the pioneers who staked their claims with eager anticipation. The heat of dry summers challenged their tenacity, while the wicked winds of winter confined them shiveringly to sodhouses and shanties.

The Great Dakota Boom of the 1880s drastically changed the face of the once unpopulated prairie. Railroad agents and town developers conducted extensive promotion campaigns, sending bundles of pamphlets and posters that extolled Dakota Territory in glowing terms to Norway, Sweden, Bohemia and other potential sources of immigrants. Representatives traveled to Europe to spread the message of cheap, bountiful acreages to land-poor farmers.

A spirit of optimism and eagerness prevailed as trainloads of settlers poured into the region. For a time there was a literal traffic jam of people in Huron, all needing food, accommodations and a means of transportation with which to begin the search for a farm site. The bustling scene was repeated at Mitchell, Aberdeen and other smaller (but no less hopeful) towns like Kimball, Plankinton,

"The Prairie Is My Garden" is artist Harvey Dunn's acknowledged masterpiece. Reproductions of the classic painting hang in the homes and offices of many former South Dakotans for whom it is a reminder of their heritage—as it was for Dunn when he painted it. South Dakota Art Museum

Woonsocket and Ipswich.

The northern tier of counties attracted great numbers of Germans from Russia, fleeing the harsh reversal of policies affecting their living conditions in the Crimea. These mislabeled "Rooshians" found a new haven in Dakota where their agricultural expertise soon turned the native prairie into vast fields of grain. For a time, Eureka in McPherson County was reputed to be one of the largest wheat shipping centers in the world with twenty or more elevators in operation.

Elsewhere in the early 1880s a few black freedmen filed claims in Sully County. Later they were joined by other ex-slaves until there were almost 400 blacks in the vicinity of Onida. Sad to say, the pressures of bias, isolation and hard times eventually took their toll and the colony eroded away. White-sheeted bigots of the Ku Klux Klan were facts of history in South Dakota, too—but certainly not commendable ones.

With stoneboats drawn by horse and oxen, farmers of all nationalities cleared their fields of rocks, fulfilled tree claim requirements by planting groves of cottonwoods and boxelders and ultimately moved their families out of shacks and dugouts into fine farm homes.

Unfortunately the challenge of the prairie didn't miraculously end. Voracious grasshoppers returned at intervals and there were years when the rains refused to fall. The disastrous "children's blizzard" of 1888 became an historic reminder of how fierce a Dakota winter storm could be. There were wind-blown grass fires and tornadoes, too, but the dauntless folks survived and developed an unspoken pride in their persistence.

In 1892 the "world's only" Corn Palace at Mitchell was unveiled as a fitting symbol of the new state's agricultural underpinning. At the South Dakota State Fair in Huron, products of the soil, barnyard and kitchen were proudly displayed as evidence of the successful conquest of nature. Years later the South Dakota Art Museum in Brookings featured "The Prairie Is My Garden," the masterpiece of artist Harvey Dunn that graphically portrayed the toughness and tenderness of a homesteading life.

The role of women on the prairie frontier—which many of Dunn's paintings dramatically depicted—was especially difficult and drudgerous. As they overcame a lack of privacy, female companionship and the niceties of any kind (even a bath was a luxury), the homesteaders' wives were true heroines of the pioneer period. They bore their children, often under the crudest circumstances, tended gardens and flocks of chickens, tried desperately to make livable homes of shacks and soddies and were the unsung champions of churches and schools. With indomitable strength, they persisted and eventually brought the refinements of family life to the raw existence that greeted them when they first arrived in Dakota.

Gradually, the once treeless, roadless plainsland became dotted with thriving villages, towns and farmsteads. Artesian wells by the hundreds brought desperately needed water. Railroads provided food items and fineries that were once a rarity. Autos replaced horses; and before and after World War I there were periods of prosperity which, for many, finally turned dreams into reality.

But there were challenges yet to come. During the Dirty Thirties, drouth, grasshoppers, a livestock-destroying disease called anthrax and a national depression all combined to force even some of the most tenacious from the land. Then, after World War II, the tearing up of hundreds of miles of railroad tracks isolated numerous small towns, some of which withered and died, while others—dependent on trucks and automobiles—struggled to survive.

When South Dakota's first century of statehood was completed, the citizens of its panoramic prairie continued to adjust to changing patterns: of larger farms, consolidated schools, shopping malls and an aging population. The challenges were new, but in a different way, the pioneering spirit remained.

Hutterite children of the Elm Springs Colony near Mitchell inspect a barnful of yellow-fluffed baby geese. Though it represents a small portion of the state's agricultural income, South Dakota has been the number one producer of geese in the nation. South Dakota Tourism, Paul Horsted photo

Steam-threshing jamborees are popular nostalgic events in South Dakota. Prairie Village, a rebuilt 1890s town near Madison, features restored agricultural equipment of another era in an annual show. Clyde Goin collection

The Sioux Falls Stockyards, with gross annual receipts that have topped the $500 million mark, provides a marketing outlet for the cattle, hogs and sheep of South Dakota ranchers and farmers. Adjacent to it, the huge John Morrell Packing Company, established in 1909, is a major processor of meat products and has been one of the state's largest employers. South Dakota Tourism

Even though the number of South Dakota farmers has dwindled through the years, many of the country churches built in the first half of the century remain well-kept and in use, a testimonial to the priorities of the rural residents. The Zion Lutheran Church near Volin is a typical example. South Dakota Magazine

South Dakota farmers have experimented with numerous crop varieties through the years, always searching for that special plant that is best suited to both the environment and the world marketplace. None have matched a field of nodding sunflowers for color and beauty. South Dakota Tourism

Home

The prairie art of Harvey Thomas Dunn, a native of Kingsbury County, captured the spirit of early-day South Dakota. Though he lived most of his life in the East, the famed illustrator for The Saturday Evening Post *and other major magazines never lost touch with his roots on Redstone Creek south of Manchester. A large collection of his pioneer paintings— which he bequeathed "to the people of South Dakota in perpetuity"—is on permanent display in the South Dakota Art Museum in Brookings. Dunn died in 1952 at the age of 68. South Dakota Art Museum*

Buffalo Bones Plowed Under

Harvey Dunn's prairie paintings were produced over a period of many years by the famed artist-illustrator when he wasn't working on commercial assignments. They were primarily for his own gratification and a personal desire to capture on canvas the heritage of his birthplace. Because he feared the fleeting impact of his magazine illustrations, they were also his hope for lasting recognition of his talent. The scenes were mostly from his memory: buffalo bones that he himself plowed under; romping home after school in Esmond Township; recalling the required patience of cow and milker; and remembering, too, the tenacity of those who called their soddies, dugouts and claim shacks "home." South Dakota Art Museum

Patience

After School

The towering Campanile is the showpiece of the campus of South Dakota State University in Brookings. It was built in 1929 as a gift of Charles Coughlin, a 1909 graduate of the school. *South Dakota State Historical Society*

Kids and the prairie are a magnificent match. Late in her life, South Dakota's most famous pioneer girl, Laura Ingalls Wilder, penned: "I can still plainly see the grass and the trees and the path winding ahead, flecked with sunshine..." *South Dakota Magazine*

Beginning with John Philip Sousa and his famous band in 1904, many entertainment celebrities have performed on the Corn Palace stage through the years. Among them have been William Jennings Bryan, Bob Hope, Red Skelton, Tennessee Ernie Ford and the locally popular Lawrence

Welk. Despite the concerns of the war in Europe, the 1917 festival (left) was well attended. The design theme of the unique domed structure in Mitchell is changed annually. *Clyde Goin collection, above, left; South Dakota Tourism, above, right*

Before railroad lines were extended, freighting companies used ox trains to move supplies cross-country to the Black Hills from such railheads and steamboat ports as Chamberlain, Fort Pierre, Bismarck and Chadron, Nebraska. This unusual wide-angle photograph was taken in 1885. South Dakota State Historical Society*

THE
BLUE BLANKET VALLEY!
Reached by way
OF
Lebanon, Potter County, Dakota.

Openings for Business Men !

CHOICE LANDS AT REASONABLE PRICES !

GOOD WATER & AN ABUNDANCE OF IT

THE CROPS in this Valley have always been good. The farmers are thrifty and although the valley has only been settled four years there are many settlers in and around Lebanon.

Corn, Wheat, Oats, Barley and Potatoes give good yields, as our farmers will testify. All kinds of Live Stock can be raised here to good advantage and profit.

Hay--Range and Water, abundant.

RAILROADS and SCHOOLS

Not a life nor a limb has been lost by frost or storm in Potter County this winter.

THE
TOWN OF LEBANON !
Is Twelve Weeks old,

and although settled late in the fall, has 30 business houses,

Lebanon is surrounded by a first-class settlement. From its principal street you can see with the naked eye over 125 farm houses. In no part of Dakota will you find a more prosperous lot of farmers.

Our merchants and business men have plenty to do, are not afraid of competition, and guarantee you a business opening in almost any line of business.

→Good Water can be Obtained by Digging Fifteen Feet.←

A GOOD OPENING FOR A FLOURING MILL.

We are not booming for a metropolis, but we do claim the best trading point in Potter county. If you have energy and business ability with a little capital, you can be sure of a snug cosy business right here.

Your investment need not be large, but it will be safe. Merchants, livery men, mechanics, harness makers, shoe makers and professional men are invited to come and see this town. Farmers can get good lands from $3 to $7 per acre. The hardships of pioneer life are largely past. The country has been tested. It shows for itself. Come and help us build a town. No matter what your business, trade or occupation, you will find a fair chance here. Don't expect too much, but come and see. It don't take a fortune to buy a town lot in Lebanon. You can get prices and terms that are reasonable.

See our large circulars for further information, or write to

CHAS. W. SEARIGHT, Town Site Agent,
LEBANON, POTTER COUNTY, DAKOTA.

Railroad and town-site companies sent a steady stream of posters, pamphlets and newspapers back east and to Europe, all extolling the virtues of Dakota and the endless opportunities available to farmers and business men. South Dakota State Historical Society

A Huron dandy was photographed with his buggy and steed in front of the Masonic Temple under construction in 1910. Owners had intense pride in their carriage horses, which were status symbols like some later-day automobiles. Dakotaland Museum

Life in the crude huts and hovels of pioneer South Dakotans was one of cramped quarters, little privacy and great boredom. Decks of cards were worn out from playing endless games of euchre and whist; and what newspapers or books were available were read and re-read until they were dog-eared and tattered. Friends of the Middle Border Museum, below; South Dakota State Historical Society, right

Schools on the prairie were anything but pretentious. What was most important to the homesteaders was providing an education for their children, regardless of conditions. Sometimes even a crude sod house with anchored roof had to do (left). In the Deadman Valley School in Stanley County, pupils learned the three R's in a log hut. Wall Drug Store collection, left; South Dakota State Historical Society, below

In Huron the "ultimate" in educational facilities was reached in 1883 when the Illinois Street High School was erected. Elementary students also learned their lessons in the ornate structure. Dakotaland Museum

The Hard Winter of 1880-81 ranks as the worst in the state's history. The snow started coming in mid-October and successive storms piled on new layers until the following March. Hundreds of new settlers were caught ill-prepared for the severe weather. Trainloads of fuel were stranded and lay buried on sidings throughout the long months as attempts to free trains along the new lines were largely unsuccessful. Agricultural Heritage Museum

Even before statehood, motorized road transportation was introduced to the region in the form of E. S. Callihan's steam-drive "autocycle," (right). The inventor, who was photographed while demonstrating his three-wheeler in Woonsocket in 1884, had come to Sanborn County just years earlier in a covered wagon. Despite this pioneering venture, however, it was well past the turn of the century before automobiles became more than an object of curiosity. Among the first to come to South Dakota were high-wheelers, manufactured by Sears Roebuck, International Harvester and other companies. They were designed to churn through the rutted dirt roads of the period. South Dakota State Historical Society

De Smet in Kingsbury County is the "Little House on the Prairie" featured in the books by Laura Ingalls Wilder. The future author was photographed in the early 1880s with her sisters, Mary (center) and Carrie (left). Now a museum, the house of Ma and Pa Ingalls, above, attracts hundreds of visitors each year, many of them children who have read the Wilder stories or seen the show based on her works on television.
South Dakota Tourism, above;
Laura Ingalls Wilder Memorial Society, Inc., right

Post offices were established in huts, dugouts and sod houses during pioneer days. Many of the early ones eventually disappeared and their postmarks became prizes for collectors. Drakola was a classic example. South Dakota State Historical Society

Picture postcards provided lasting visual records of numerous South Dakota towns in their earlier years. Platte in Charles Mix County (right) was settled in 1882 in a region heavily populated by Hollanders. The town already boasted a street light when this photo was taken in 1910. Miller in Hand County, above, was named for Henry Miller, an early settler. Like many towns, its main street remained unpaved until the horseless carriage proved it was here to stay. Yankton County Historical Society, right; Scott Heidepriem collection, above

Six oared boat race on the famous Lake Prior. Woonsocket, S.D.

The town of Woonsocket in Sanborn County has several distinctions. It once boasted the world's most powerful artesian well, which sent a stream rocketing 96 feet into the air. The area's subterranean water source maintained the town's Lake Prior, once known for its boat races, above, and other recreational activities. Charles W. Post supposedly had selected Woonsocket as the site for his cereal company, but when he was refused free land for his factory, he built a Battle Creek, Mich., instead. St. Wilfrid's Catholic Church, right, is pictured beyond the lake named for Charles H. Prior, who was the land agent when the town was founded. He named it after Woonsocket, R.I. Clyde Goin collection, right; Yankton County Historical Society, above

Plankinton was first called Merrill when it was settled in 1880. When the Milwaukee Road arrived, the town was renamed for John H. Plankinton, a Chicago meat-packer. In the distribution of the various state institutions by the legislature, Plankinton was awarded the State Training School. It also was designated the county seat of Aurora County. The court house is shown in 1908 behind the local fishing hole. Robert E. Kolbe collection

The Chicago and North Western's bridge over the James River near Huron was the company's major engineering challenge east of the Missouri. Daily trains were the lifeblood of growing South Dakota cities when this photo was taken in 1911. Dick Crabb collection

As a principal Missouri River crossing, Mobridge became a busy railroad center. Its role changed, however, as trains were replaced by trucks; and—with the damming of the river and the creation of Lake Oahe—recreation developed as a key industry for the town. Mobridge Tribune

Farmers were proud of their horses, no matter what size. At Ipswich, J. W. Parmley raised Percherons and Shetland ponies. South Dakota State Historical Society

Cigar stores were popular gathering places for men in the early 1900s. The shop of this Pierre merchant was typical of the business places of the era. The stove was usually the focal point— and occasionally the cause of fires in the wooden frame buildings. South Dakota State Historical Society

Whistlestop visits by politicians were quite common when railroad passenger service was available throughout most of the state. At Miller in Hand County, President William Howard Taft drew an admiring crowd in the early 1900s. Scott Heidepriem collection

As mechanical equipment—like the Deering header, left—was introduced, grain fields got larger, and more elevators had to be built along the rail lines to handle the yield. Wheat was king in the northern counties, although barley, oats, rye and flax were among the crops harvested by homesteaders. South Dakota State Historical Society

Water for towns, farms and the insatiable thirst of locomotives kept well-drillers in constant demand throughout the state. An artesian aquifer underlying most east-river counties produced free-flowing gushers until the excessive drilling greatly reduced subterranean pressure. Beginning in the early 1880s, hundreds of new wells tapped the source each year, reaching a peak in 1914 when at least 500 were drilled. South Dakota State University

South Dakota depended on horsepower
from real horses for construction, agriculture and drayage until well after World
War I. The P. J. Schuchart Transfer Line
of Pierre was a typical operation. South
Dakota State Historical Society

When Fort Hale on the Missouri River
opposite the mouth of Crow Creek was
abandoned, entrepreneurs at Chamberlain
dismantled the main structure and moved
it down river on the ice in 1890. Once in
the Brule County town, they rebuilt it and
named it the Hotel Taft. Chamberlain
Register collection

The Mitchell Corn Palace festival was first staged in 1892, but because of drouth and hard times it didn't catch on as an annual event until 1902. Decorating the building with South Dakota-grown grain has become an unusual art form as new designs are created each year. Workmen used crude scaffolding as they prepared this first palace, above, for the gala autumn event. The 1893 show featured the brass band of Lynn, Massachusetts, below. Clyde Goin collection

Carnivals and street events have always been a part of the Corn Palace festival. The unique grain-bedecked structure is located at the far end of Mitchell's main street in this early 1900s photograph. Robert E. Kolbe collection

Ferry boats were used for excursions as well as cross-river travel. In 1904 when Pierre was involved in its final election fight to retain the state capital, thousands of visitors were taken on tours and otherwise entertained to win their votes to beat back Mitchell's challenge. South Dakota State Historical Society, left; Wall Drug Store collection, below

The cornerstone of the state capitol was laid on June 25, 1908, with construction beginning shortly afterward. This photo shows not only the work in progress but also, in the background, how undeveloped Pierre was at the time. Codington County Historical Society

A pre-World War I biplane flew over a Chicago and North Western passenger train and the state capitol after its dedication, signifying a bright future for the small, centrally located city of Pierre. By then, its citizens had thwarted several attempts to move the seat of government elsewhere. South Dakota State Historical Society

Steam traction and horse power combined forces in the paving of Huron's Dakota Avenue in 1916. Daum's Auditorium was in the background. Dakotaland Museum

South Dakota's tourism industry began to develop in the 1920s. Cabin camps—the predecessors of later-day motels—offered dollar-a-night accommodations for the hardy travelers of mostly dirt and graveled roads. Typical facilities of the period were those at Chamberlain (right) and Spearfish (below). Chamberlain Register *collection, right; Clyde Goin collection, below*

Rail transportation was vital to the early development of South Dakota, but with so many trains on the move, it was not without an occasional accident. In September of 1925, the fireman of this Milwaukee Road locomotive (above) was scalded to death when the engine hit a cow on the track two miles east of Chamberlain. Less serious was this collision (right), one of numerous derailments that occurred because of such problems as faulty switching and unstable roadbeds. Friends of the Middle Border Museum, above; Yankton County Historical Society, right

Going to country school in South Dakota sometimes meant long walks or pony rides in the era before sophisticated buses and changing attitudes. These Walworth County children were not unlike their counterparts in other sections of the state where the one-room rural school house was the accepted means of education. South Dakota State Historical Society

In the days before heavily restricted limits on pheasants and waterfowl, photographs like this were the proud boasts of successful hunters in South Dakota. Visiting nimrods have provided the state with millions of dollars in revenue through the years. South Dakota Game, Fish and Parks Department

Among South Dakota's larger game animals are pronghorn antelopes. These orphans from the Slim Buttes area were moved to the State Fair grounds in Huron where they had to be bottle fed. Clyde Goin collection

During the Dirty Thirties, two New Deal programs—the Public Works Administration and the Works Progress Administration—financed the construction of numerous public buildings and roads across the state. Farmers were paid for their own labor and the use of their horses to help them through the worst of the depression. Clyde Goin collection

Tenacious though they were, many South Dakota farmers and townspeople gave up the fight during the drouth and depression of the Dirty Thirties. Most headed westward with their meager belongings to Oregon, Washington and California, hoping to make a new start without dust and grasshoppers. South Dakota State Historical Society

These before and after pictures of a Beadle County farm near Wolsey show the quick recovery from the effects of drouth and dust storms in the Dirty Thirties. In two years, plantings of cane and sudan grass—with the help of a little rain—replaced dirt drifts and tumbleweeds. U.S. Department of Agriculture

The Young Citizens League was an active patriotic and educational organization in many South Dakota schools prior to World War II. Students learned about the workings of government, and a convention at the state capital was an especially memorable experience. Clyde Goin collection

South Dakota farm wives, from pioneering days on, have been noted for their hoards of canned fruits, vegetables and even meat. Preparing for possible "hard times" was as important as day-to-day chores. Women proudly exhibited their efforts in county competitions and at the State Fair in Huron. South Dakota State University

Vestiges of South Dakota's past are evident in the still visible wagon train ruts on the prairie (top), the foundations of pioneer settlements (left), and the remnants of military installations like Fort Randall in Gregory County, which was established in 1856. Sitting Bull was once imprisoned there, but only crumbling ruins of the post chapel remain. Black Hills, Badlands & Lakes Association, top; Clyde Goin collection, left; South Dakota State Historical Society, above

Considered by some to be slightly off the beaten path, South Dakota enjoys only infrequent visits by U.S. presidents. Through the years, residents of Pierre have greeted William Howard Taft (right); Calvin Coolidge with Governor William J. Bulow (below, center); Franklin D. Roosevelt and son James, who were hosted by then Senator Bulow and Governor Tom Berry on the president's right (bottom); and John F. Kennedy with Governor Archie Gubbrud and Senator George McGovern at the dedication of Oahe Dam (opposite page). South Dakota State Historical Society

Canada geese and other waterfowl winter in the geothermally heated lake next to the state capitol in Pierre. The centrally located city on the Missouri River became the temporary seat of government after a state-wide balloting in 1889. A year later it received the permanent designation after a bitter, expensive election in which Huron was the other contender. Pierre backers had to fight off one more challenge in 1904 when Mitchell was outvoted 58,617 to 41,155.

Modeled after the Montana capitol at Helena, South Dakota's statehouse was officially dedicated on June 30, 1910, during the first term of Governor Robert S. Vessey. The architects were C. E. Bell and M. S. Detweiler of Minneapolis, while O. H. Olsen of Stillwater, Minnesota, outbid South Dakota builders for the general contract. The building was constructed mainly of Ortonville granite and Bedford stone from Indiana, although native field boulders were used in the foundation. The total cost, including landscaping, was $951,000. South Dakota Tourism

Goodlands & Badlands

Between the Missouri River and the Black Hills lies South Dakota's "short-grass country," where farms become ranches measured in thousands of acres and a fierce spirit of independence prevails among those who live where population and rainfall are equally sparse.

It is truly a land of cowboys and Indians, although vast fields of wheat require ranchers to be as much at home in the cab of a giant tractor as they are in the saddle. Adaptability to great distances from schools, churches, hospitals and grocery stores is still a required trait for those South Dakotans who prefer stretching room to big-city clutter and traffic. They gladly exchange creature conveniences for freedom of movement and the unique beauty of grand sunrises and spectacular sunsets.

While the Great Dakota Boom brought thousands of homesteaders to the region east of the Missouri, there was relatively little interest in settlement on the Great Sioux Reserve during that period. On the other hand, cattle interests were attracted to the "oceans of grass" on the fenceless plains of the public domain. The discovery of gold in the Black Hills created a sudden demand for beef by hungry prospectors, but more important for continuing prosperity were the markets of the east.

To reach the slaughter houses of Chicago and elsewhere, tens of thousands of grass-fattened animals crossed the Missouri on pontoon bridges and ferry boats to railheads at Pierre, Chamberlain, Evarts and Le Beau. Huge cattle companies—like the Matador of Texas—dominated the industry; and one syndicate headed by G. E. "Ed" Lemmon leased and fenced an area said to be larger than the state of Rhode Island. Other famous cattlemen of the era were James "Scotty" Philip, Harry Oelrichs and Murdo McKenzie, who, like Lemmon, had towns named after them.

In 1907, the long awaited railroad race from the Missouri to the Black Hills took place, signaling the end of stage-coach and freight wagon traffic. The Chicago and North Western from Pierre and the Milwaukee Road from Chamber-

South Dakota Tourism, Paul Horsted photo

lain both reached Rapid City in July of that year. Three months later the Milwaukee's northern line crossed the river at Mobridge and was extended westward to Lemmon. After that, rail cars came to the cattle instead of the other way around.

An influx of homesteaders followed the track-laying, and government-sponsored land lotteries on the various Indian reservations attracted thousands of potential claimants. As in the eastern half of the state, small towns sprang up along the rights-of-way, although the seven-to ten-mile rule did not generally apply in the west-river country, where it soon became evident that soil and limited rainfall precluded small crop-farming operations.

In contrast to the shortgrass "goodlands" that range from the pine-covered ridges in the south to the northern border beyond the Grand River is a most unusual geographic feature. Lt. Col. George Armstrong Custer called it "hell with the fire burned out." The grotesquely beautiful formations of the White River Badlands were created by the relentless forces of erosion over a period of more than a million years. The sculpted landscape is now a 244,000-acre national park. Its revealed secrets of aeons past include fossils of prehistoric camels, hippopotami, three kinds of rhinoceroses, oreodons (ruminating pigs) and various other extinct species.

One of the new 1907 railroad towns was located at the north "wall" of the Badlands. Its prospects for the future were not much greater than those of other isolated whistlestops until Ted and Dorothy Hustead began giving away free ice water to travelers who visited their Wall Drug Store during the Dirty Thirties. It was the beginning of one of South Dakota's most successful private ventures and best known tourist attractions. The Husteads proved that, with hard work and a little imagination, dreams could still be realized in the shortgrass country.

In the northwest corner of the state, a few scattered oil wells have generated guarded optimism about a possible hidden bonanza. The discovery of buried petrified trees in Perkins County led to the founding of a jewelry industry at Lemmon. Farther east, lignite coal deposits in the vicinity of Firesteel— which provided fuel for needy families during the Great Depression—still await the means and usages to make them profitable.

In Harding County, a range of pine-topped hills and jagged limestone cliffs stretches more than 30 miles from its northern extremity to a geographic punctuation mark at the southern end known as Sheep Mountain. These are the Slim Buttes, where in 1876—after the Custer massacre at Little Big Horn— cavalry troopers under Gen. George Crook engaged in an indecisive skirmish with an Indian force. It was the closest thing to a real battle ever fought in South Dakota. Far more dramatic is the legend of Hugh Glass, who survived a hand-to-hand fight with a grizzly bear near the fork of the Grand River in 1823.

Mostly, though, the broad expanse between the Missouri River and the Black Hills is a land of unsung heroes of the past: of cowboys and honyockers, courageous women, horse-and-buggy doctors, teachers in one-room school houses, printer-editors of flimsy newspapers and the priests and preachers who served them in their times of joy and sadness.

The Badlands, though desolate and arid, lack not for color, either from the play of the sun on shaded layers of soil and sand or from the summer wild flowers that bravely take root in the valleys. Literally millions of photographs have been taken of the unusual formations, and, like fingerprints, no two seem to be alike. South Dakota Tourism, Paul Horsted photos

A dead-end Butte County road leads travelers to the geographic center of the 50 United States. The site is about 17 miles west of Castle Rock between Dead Horse Creek and Willow Creek. *South Dakota Tourism*

Bison dusting themselves or grazing peacefully on a hillside are tempting sights for tourists with cameras. However, the docile-appearing animals are swifter and more dangerous than they appear, so visitors to South Dakota parks are repeatedly warned to enjoy the view but to stay in their cars! *South Dakota Tourism, Paul Horsted photo*

Rodeo has long been South Dakota's leading professional sport. Youngsters begin at the minor league level—the Little Britches and high school events—and dream of one day competing on the pro circuit where Casey Tibbs, a state hero, made it big. *South Dakota Tourism*

The annual Governor's Pheasant Hunt has been a fall tradition in South Dakota. In 1987 Governor George S. Mickelson (front row, orange vest) used the opportunity to promote the state's obvious outdoor attributes while also stressing to corporate guests the good business climate of the state. Mickelson was preceded by his father, George T., as South Dakota's chief executive. The younger Mickelson's middle name, Speaker, was given to him by a resolution of the State House of Representatives when his father was serving in that position. South Dakota Tourism, Paul Horsted photo

The cattle drive has been a South Dakota tradition for more than a century. Cowboys once moved vast herds of longhorns across the Great Sioux Reserve. Later-day ranchers in the shortgrass country still use horses to shift Herefords, Angus and various exotic breeds from pasture to pasture in the old-fashioned way. South Dakota Tourism

A buried forest of petrified wood and large quantities of fossilized remains of 50-million-year-old plant and animal life have been found in Perkins County. At Lemmon—named for pioneer cattleman G. E. "Ed" Lemmon—a Petrified Wood Park features an unusual collection of these prehistoric natural relics. A jewelry manufacturing industry was started in the town because of the availability of beautiful, variegated specimens. South Dakota Tourism

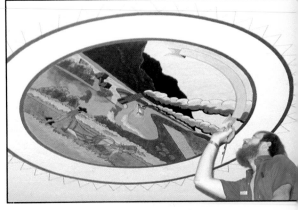

Beginning in the mid-1980s, an extensive restoration project was undertaken at the state capitol in Pierre so that it would be ready for the South Dakota centennial in 1989. Original wall and ceiling art of the 1912 structure was given special attention, including retouching of the state seal. The state's motto in the seal—"Under God the People Rule"—was written by Reverend Joseph Ward, founder of Yankton College. He died at 51, nine days after President Benjamin Harrison signed the admission proclamation on November 2, 1889. South Dakota Tourism

A South Dakota cowgirl enjoys a sunset at the corral gate of the Double-S Ranch near Cedar Butte. Where women once appeared only in gingham dress, they now engage in herd-riding, branding operations, calf-roping and other chores that were thought to be exclusively he-man activities. South Dakota Tourism

*Friends called him a mover-and-shaker;
foes said he was a political tyrant.
Whatever the label, when William Janklow
served as governor from 1978 to 1986, he
was South Dakota's busiest promoter.
Typical was this pose at the governor's
mansion in Pierre to publicize a Black
Hills Corvette Classic. When he left office,
Janklow had served as governor longer than
anyone in the state's history. South Dakota
Tourism*

*Although Doc Brewster Higley wrote
"Home on the Range" at his Kansas homestead, South Dakota can also claim to be a
land "where the deer and the antelope
play." The entire state has large populations of both whitetail and mule deer, the
latter being largely confined to the west-
river country. South Dakota Tourism,
Paul Horsted photo*

*Hikers and bikers enjoy the ups and downs
of Badlands National Park, a 244,000-
acre moonscape carved some 35 million
years ago by wind and water. South Dakota
Tourism, Paul Horsted photo*

124

Reminiscent of the Oklahoma land rushes, the opening of the Great Sioux Reserve in 1890 attracted large crowds of land-seekers, many of them speculators. Near Pierre, this group waited at the starting line ready for the race to the most desirable claims. Later the government devised a lottery system to replace the first-come-first-served stampedes. *South Dakota State Historical Society*

In the summer of 1823, Hugh Glass—a guide for a trading expedition headed by General William A. Ashley—was scouting ahead of the party in what became Perkins County when he was attacked by a grizzly bear. Companions who were with him ran away and reported him dead. Though his leg was broken and he was severely clawed, Hugh somehow survived, and the story of his incredible hundred-mile journey back to the nearest settlement is one of South Dakota's most fascinating legends. *Federal Writers' Project, 1938*

Wherever a homesteading rush occurred, tiny newspapers were started to take advantage of the final-proof advertising required by the law. The only equipment needed was a "shirt tail full of type" and a crude hand press. This husband and wife team published the short-lived Caton Advertiser in Meade County. Their operation was in an unpretentious office building. *South Dakota State Historical Society*

The town of Fort Pierre developed on the site of a trading post established in 1832 by Pierre Chouteau, Jr., after whom it was named. In later years it became a shipping point and supply center for the cattle ranchers of the area. Replenishing chuck wagons was a profitable business for local merchants. South Dakota State Historical Society

Minnesela (below) was once the county seat of Butte County. However, when the Fremont, Elkhorn and Missouri Valley Railroad built north from Whitewood in 1890, the company established its own town of Belle Fourche three and a half miles away. Despite efforts by residents of Minnesela to thwart the railroad's efforts, the final results were inevitable, and another ghost town was created. Town founders pose on the balcony of the Minnesela Hotel (left) during its brief period of glory. South Dakota State Historical Society

B Troop of the 7th Cavalry Regiment stood for inspection on January 18, 1891, some three weeks after participating in the massacre at Wounded Knee Creek. The highly controversial event—called a "battle" by the U.S. Army—was in reality a deplorable slaughter in which an undetermined number of Indians, including infants, were killed and unceremoniously buried in a mass grave. The official surgeon's report noted that the 7th Cavalry lost one officer and 29 enlisted men. A similar number were wounded. South Dakota State Historical Society

Treeless and stark against the prairie sky, the Dewey County town of Firesteel (right) had a uniquenes of its own. A large deposit of lignite was discovered nearby, and hopes for a coal-mining industry blossomed. After a quarter century of off-and-on production by several private operators, the state opened a strip mine in the winter of 1933-34 to provide fuel for needy families. The experiment proved a financial bust when it was determined that coal could be purchased elsewhere for much less than it cost to mine it. The east side of the town's main street (above) included a general store, a meat market and a restaurant. Timber Lake and Area Historical Society, Frank Cundill photo, right; Leon Gifford photo, above

While life in a sod-reinforced claim shanty or a hillside dugout lacked most of the comforts of human existence, sometimes all it took was a little music to overcome the boredom and loneliness. Fiddlers and concertina players were always in demand on the frontier for dances, wedding parties and other celebrations. South Dakota State Historical Society

Like many other homesteaders, George E. Pope took advantage of the prairie sod to erect his first house at Herrick in Gregory County. The date was undoubtedly 1904, when the lottery for unalloted lands on the Rosebud Reservation took place. Wall Drug Store collection

Evarts, located on the Missouri River in Walworth County, was once considered to be one of the world's largest primary shipping points for cattle. Animals fattened on huge ranches were trailed to the river through "The Strip," a six-mile wide, 80-mile long corridor between the Standing Rock and Cheyenne River Reservations. By ferry boat and pontoon bridge they crossed the river to the railhead for shipment to Chicago and other eastern markets. When the railroads extended their lines beyond the Missouri, Evarts—shown here in its heyday—was by-passed and became a ghost town. W. H. Over Museum, above; South Dakota State Historical Society, left

129

The various openings of Indian lands were heavily promoted by the railroads. Dozens of special trains brought thousands of land-seekers to the registration sites for government lotteries. South Dakota State Historical Society

ISN'T IT TIME YOU OWNED A FARM?

THREE THOUSAND GOVERNMENT HOMESTEADS

IN THE

Pine Ridge and Rosebud Indian Reservations

DIRECT ROUTE TO

GREGORY, DALLAS AND RAPID CITY

WHICH ARE POINTS OF REGISTRATIONS

Time of Registration, October 2 to 21, 1911

Buffalo teams in harness were symbolic of the passing of a historic era. Faster and more agile than they look and possessing an unpredictable temperament, the once-great lords of the plains were subject to domestication by only the bravest or the most foolhardy. South Dakota State Historical Society, below; Wall Drug Store collection, left

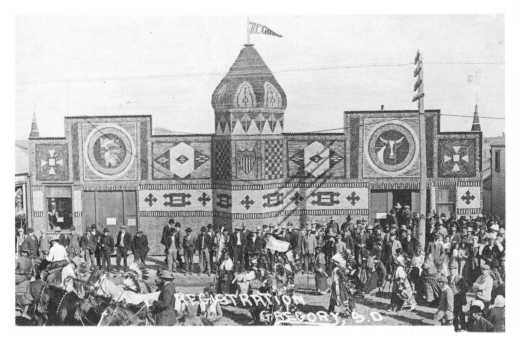

Plankinton had a Grain Palace in 1892 (below), the same year the "world's only Corn Palace" was opened in Mitchell. The Plankinton effort was short-lived as was a similar building in Gregory (right), where land openings on the Rosebud Reservation attracted thousands of registrants. Clyde Goin collection

The Timber Lake Grain Palace never caught on like Mitchell's gaudy showplace, but at least for one year prior to World War I, it indicated pride in the agricultural production of the region. Timber Lake and Area Historical Society, Frank Cundill photo

Thousands of hopeful applicants flocked to the boom town of Dallas in 1908 to register for the government lottery for homesteads in the second Rosebud opening. At one time, the namesake of the Texas metropolis boasted a three-block business district, seven churches and a proportionate number of saloons, but the glory days didn't last and the dwindling town struggled to stay alive. Robert E. Kolbe collection

In the Dewey County village of Promise, this youngster showed some promise of his own as a future cowboy—or maybe a jockey. For the town itself, the hopes went unfulfilled and its site eventually was covered by the backwaters of the Oahe Dam. Timber Lake and Area Historical Society, Frank Cundill photo

The quest for water was a constant challenge on the plains. Early settlers often had to haul it by the barrelful from lakes and streams until crude drilling rigs like this one were able to provide wells closer to home. Timber Lake and Area Historical Society, Frank Cundill photo

Life on a treeless claim in Indian reservation country could not be construed as living in a land of luxury—but the overriding optimism of most homesteaders generally overcame the bleakness and boredom. It would paint an erroneous picture, however, to overlook the occasional suicides and commitments to the State Insane Asylum at Yankton, as South Dakota's mental institution was then known, which were attributable to the isolation that some settlers were not prepared for. Timber Lake and Area Historical Society, Frank Cundill photo

Dakota Territory's first legislature in 1862
enacted a Marks and Brands Law that
permitted ranchers to record their brands
with the county register of deeds for a fee of
25 cents. Thereafter, the branding of cattle
and horses became an annual ritual as a
protection against rustlers and for the
return of strays. South Dakota State
Historical Society, top; Timber Lake and
Area Historical Society, Frank Cundill
photo, bottom

An enterprising merchant in Belle Fourche advertised his emporium for all to see above the town's wide main street. The Butte County seat had almost a movie set appearance, complete with wooden sidewalks and hitching rails. Clyde Goin collection

Sitting tall in the saddle on a whiteface steer would seem to be detrimental to a real cowboy's image, but these rodeo riders apparently thought it would at least be an interesting experience and maybe worth a few laughs. Timber Lake and Area Historical Society, Frank Cundill photo

In sparsely populated Jones County, Westover—south of Murdo on the White River—never grew beyond the hamlet stage. It had a recorded population of five in 1940, and its post office was eventually closed in 1957. Winifred Reutter photo

Town leaders promoted the west-river country as the "last great frontier" when it eventually was opened for settlement. The Murdo Coyote editorialized in 1907 that "The young man who has the nerve to leave the drudgery of the mill and factory and strike out for himself will succeed in the west." Center for Western Studies

The women on South Dakota homesteads had to know how to hitch and saddle, along with all their other chores. They hauled grain to town, brought home provisions and occasionally had to make emergency runs to distant neighbors to assist in delivering babies or to help an ailing wife. Bess Bristol (middle), sister of photographer Frank Cundill, who took these pictures, homesteaded in Dewey County in 1911. Timber Lake and Area Historical Society

"Flimsy little wooden towns" is what
author Hamlin Garland called South
Dakota's mushrooming prairie villages.
Bison in Perkins County was platted in
1907 shortly before this picture was taken,
and it fitted Garland's description. Wall
Drug Store collection

Eager merchants rushed to get their
buildings completed when the first sale of
townsite lots took place in Timber Lake on
August 15, 1910. The Milwaukee Road
tracks had reached the new town on the
previous May 10, and the first issue of the
Timer Lake Tribune was printed in the
following month. Clyde Goin collection

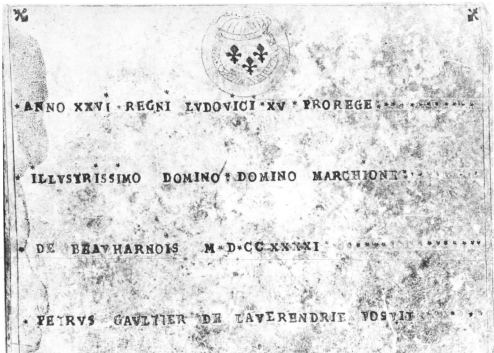

ANNO XXVI REGNI LVDOVICI XV PROREGE

ILLVSTRISSIMO DOMINO DOMINO MARCHIONE

DE BEAVHARNOIS M·D·CC·XXXXI

PETRVS GAVLTIER DE LAVERENDRIE POSVIT

In 1913 several school children discovered a lead plate on the gumbo bluffs above Fort Pierre. It turned out to be one of the most significant historical finds in South Dakota's history as the inscribed metal plate—8½ inches wide by 6½ inches high—attested to the fact that Louis Joseph and Francois la Verendrye with two companions had been on the site and had claimed the land for France. *South Dakota State Historical Society*

Pierre, S.D. from Verendrye Hill

millerpix.

139

The horseless carriage came to Philip in a big way early in the 20th century. This gathering of a wide variety of pioneer models was billed as Winter Brothers Opening Day. Robert E. Kolbe collection

Parades and street carnivals broke the monotony of prairie living. At Timber Lake (above) a civic celebration brought out Indians in full regalia, while a concessionaire offered a chance to win a doll on his wheel of fortune. Various anniversaries and holidays provided plenty of opportunities to bring out the band and follow the music down the main streets of new towns like Isabel, Faith and McLaughlin. Timber Lake and Area Historical Society, Frank Cundill photos

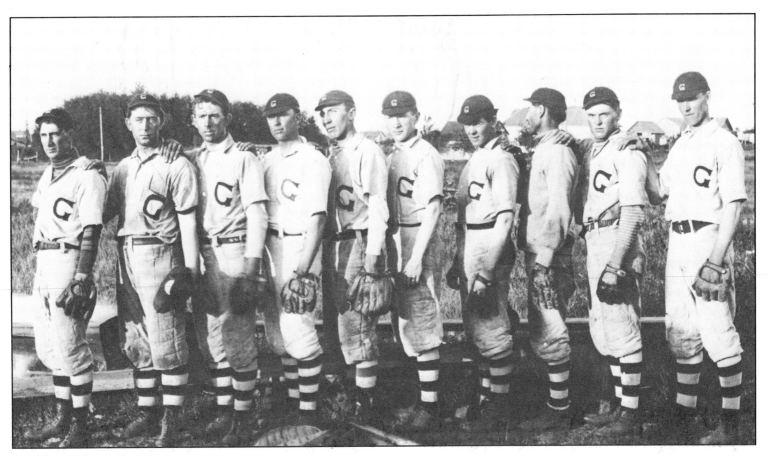

A town or community without a baseball team was a rarity in South Dakota in the early decades of the 1900s. These Gettysburg players with high-topped shoes were typical of the hometown athletes, who often played on converted pastures and other makeshift fields. Rivalries were intense, and pitchers were sometimes imported for special games. *South Dakota State Historical Society*

A patient cow and a diligent young farmhand combine to produce milk for the table and cream for the churn. Prior to World War II, most of South Dakota's small family farms had a few milk cows, a flock of chickens, several pigs and a large garden in an effort to be reasonably self-sustaining. *South Dakota State Historical Society*

Before refrigerators and ice-making machines, South Dakotans "harvested" blocks of ice from lakes and streams, storing it in layers of sawdust in whatever buildings were adaptable. This winter scene was on the Grand River in Perkins County. *South Dakota State Historical Society*

Getting out of soddies and dugouts and into two-story frame houses—with bedrooms for the children—was the dream of homesteaders on both sides of the Missouri. Many of the dwellings in the second stage of the upgrading process were constructed with shared labor as neighbors (often miles apart) came to one another's aid for barn-raisings and other tasks where "many hands made light work." Wall Drug Store collection

A pressed tin house was a virtual palace compared to the huts of some prairie homesteaders. For most pioneers, these proving-up dwellings were just temporary inconveniences until they could build the permanent farm houses that figured in their dreams when they came to Dakota. *Timber Lake and Area Historical Society, Frank Cundill photo*

Real wranglers from the plains of South Dakota bore little resemblance to the guitar-strumming drug store cowboys of a later era. These riders—and a local lawman—were photographed at the Cheyenne River Rodeo, one of many such events held throughout the state each year. *Friends of the Middle Border Museum*

Like so many other South Dakota towns, Timber Lake owed its existence to the railroad, which reached the area in the spring of 1910. Besides being the scene of many farewells and hellos, the small-town depot was a vital communications link to the rest of the world through the deft fingers of the station master on the telegraph key. *Timber Lake and Area Historical Society, Frank Cundill photo*

Photographer Frank Cundill contrived this fake holdup which he titled "Fixing a Tenderfoot." The picture was taken prior to World War I, otherwise it might be mistaken for a scene from one of the early cowboy movies of the '20s and '30s. *Timber Lake and Area Historical Society*

To be successful, every new South Dakota town had to have a newspaper, and some had two or more at the same time. Typical was the Presho Post. *Often the typesetter was a woman, and most had a young "printer's devil" as an assistant. South Dakota Press Association*

The Northwest Post, *established in 1902, eventually became the* Belle Fourche Daily Post *in 1935. Hundreds of weekly newspapers started in humble beginnings throughout the state. Some held on to become long-lasting publications; many others failed and disappeared, especially after the homestead advertising windfall was no longer available to support them. South Dakota Press Association*

A stallion named Tipperary, born in 1905 to a wild mare near Camp Crook, became a rodeo bronc in 1915 and bucked his way to immortality. From 1916 to 1921, Tipperary threw 91 riders. Only one man—movie cowboy and stuntman Yakima Canutt (in the white shirt)—successfully rode the cantankerous bay during his prime. The spirited horse died during a blizzard in 1932 and is memorialized by a monument in the Buffalo town park. South Dakota Magazine

A Farmers' Institute held in 1916 at the Corson County town of Thunder Hawk drew a big crowd. State leaders exalted the farm family, and S. A. Cochrane, who directed the institute program, wrote: "The man reared on a farm is much more likely to be a citizen who will respect and defend the laws of his country than one reared in the indolence of town life." Robert E. Kolbe collection

Band concerts in the town band shell or the city park were popular diversions of the pre-television age. The McLaughlin Band performed for picnickers in Corson County in the late 1920s. Robert E. Kolbe collection

Cowboys went to town for an occasional spree, but this heavy drinking pose was undoubtedly set up for the photographer's benefit. Range bosses didn't take too kindly to hitting the bottle when there was work to be done. Wall Drug Store collection

The life of pioneer cowboys, glamourized in movies and fiction, was instead one of drudgerous labor—riding herd, patrolling fences and branding bawling calves. They often slept under open skies, and their dining room was the prairie floor when they were on the trail or engaged in a roundup. Their gear and garb were practical and not silver-studded because they were working men—not the exciting gunslingers Hollywood made them out to be.

In South Dakota, large cattle companies flourished after the cession of the Great Sioux Reserve in 1889. They included the giant Matador of Texas with its Drag V brand, the Sheidley Company with its Flying V and A. D. Marriott's H.A.T. outfit, with three brands shaped like square, round and pointed head gear. These and smaller ranch operators—including Indians—used "The Strip" between the Standing Rock and Cheyenne River Reservations to get their cattle across the Missouri River to railheads at Evarts and La Beau. It was the heyday for cowboys, but decades later—even with barbed wire, small farm herds and giant feed lots of future generations—the working wranglers and their horses were still necessary to do what machines could not do.

Clyde Goin collection

148

Clyde Goin collection

Clyde Goin collection

Clyde Goin collection

No. 802. "A MESS SCENE." Scene
on "Round Up" of 1887 in Dakota.
(Photo, and copyright by Grabill, 1889.)

Clyde Goin collection

150

Wall Drug Store collection

South Dakota State Historical Society

Dinner On the Round Up
PL-2

South Dakota State Historical Society

Tumbleweeds and dust storms accompanied the economic doldrums of the Great Depression throughout South Dakota. The west-river plains area was especially hard hit, as evidenced by the dust drifts in the farmyard of Commissioner C. M. Olsen of Gregory County. South Dakota State Historical Society

The mute evidence of what drouth can do on the Dakota plainsland cannot be overlooked in the recording of the state's history. Harsh reminders of the Dirty Thirties, they are also symbols of the tenacity that permitted the state's farmers and ranchers to recover from such plagues of nature. South Dakota State Historical Society

For many South Dakotans the depression era was a time of struggle and despair, as evidenced by a mother's expression in this Works Progress Administration photo of 1936 (left). In Pennington County another mother could still smile despite the conditions of her humble abode (middle), while a drouth-displaced farm family headed west in an early home-made version of a mobile home (bottom). Clyde Goin collection, left; South Dakota State Historical Society, middle and bottom

Tom Berry, a working rancher from Belvidere (on the lead horse) became the state's second Democratic governor in 1932 when drouth and depression caused the state's usually Republican voters to seek a change. Berry was also the first chief executive from the west-river country and was popularly known as the "Cowboy Governor." Clyde Goin collection

Wall Drug Store, named for the eastern Pennington County town on the edge of the Badlands where it is located, is one of South Dakota's—and the nation's—most unusual success stories. When pharmacist Ted Hustead and his wife Dorothy were struggling to make a living in the Dirty Thirties, they hit on the simple idea of offering free ice water to motorists passing through their town. Later, signs announcing the number of miles to Wall Drug from far-away places including the South Pole was a gimmick that captured the imagination of tourists and travel writers. As a result, the Husteads' once quiet store became a "must" stopping place for thousands of visitors daily during the summer season. Wall Drug Store collection

Ted and Dorothy Hustead bought what was then a patent medicine store in the Pennington County town of Wall in December of 1931, as poor a time as there ever was to go into business in South Dakota. They lived with their young son, Bill, in a 20- by 24-foot area in the back of the building, separated from the pharmacy by a brown curtain. From this humble beginning, the phenomenal Wall Drug Store evolved into one of the state's greatest tourist attractions and success stories. Wall Drug Store collection

While the emphasis was on cattle in South Dakota's west-river country, the state has long been a leading producer of sheep, especially in the Belle Fourche area. Archer B. Gilfillan (below), a college-educated sheepherder in the Slim Buttes region, wrote a popular book in 1929 titled Sheep, *best known of his numerous literary efforts. This flock (right) was wintering near Vivian. South Dakota State Historical Society, below; Center for Western Studies, right*

Rattlesnakes were one of many challenges faced by west-river pioneers. One wife reported that they stuck their heads up through holes in her kitchen floor, while ranchers claimed they killed their livestock.

The problem was still there in 1937 when A. M. Jackley was appointed state rattlesnake exterminator by the South Dakota legislature. He killed uncounted numbers of rattlers. Others were trapped and

released in the wilderness or given to universities for research. He was bitten several times but died of a heart attack at age 70. Friends of the Middle Border Museum

E. Y. Berry, a former county judge and publisher of the McLaughlin Messenger, was a popular U.S. representative from the state's Second District. Here he was participating in a mock jailing during a newspaper convention in 1949. Because of its population, South Dakota eventually was limited to a single congressman. South Dakota Press Association

Casey Tibbs of Fort Pierre became an international rodeo champion. He was photographed demonstrating his bronc riding skill aboard an ill-tempered horse named "Nugget." South Dakota State Historical Society

The Slim Buttes in Harding County extend some 30 miles north and south and were so named because they are vertically slim and range generally from one to three miles in width. Isolated as they are in the northwest corner of the state, they do not get the tourist attention accorded the Black Hills and Badlands. Clyde Goin collection

Buried in the earth in five western South Dakota counties—and almost disregarded by the people living around them—have been 150 Minuteman missiles, each armed with a two-megaton nuclear bomb. This front line of America's retaliatory force is not secret to friend or foe. Two-man crews are on duty around the clock in steel-reinforced concrete launch control centers like this one shown under construction. Located in an area where the bow and arrow was once the ultimate weapon, the missiles rest in their sunken silos, with everyone involved hopeful that they will never have to be fired. Ellsworth Air Force Base

Bringing in the family Christmas tree is a tradition on many west-river ranches, as the Black Hills, the Pine Ridge country and the fringes of the Badlands offer a variety of conifers. The U.S. Forest Service also permits city-dwellers to cut their own trees in certain areas of the Black Hills if strict rules are followed. Black Hills, Badlands & Lakes Association

The castle-like cliffs of the Slim Buttes dominate the hauntingly scenic landscape of Harding County in the extreme north-west corner of the state. The picturesque region was the site of the so-called Battle of Slim Buttes, which followed Custer's demise at Little Big Horn. Black Hills, Badlands & Lakes Association

Because ranching continues to be an important state industry—especially in the west-river country—rodeos are popular events for both spectators and participants throughout South Dakota. Bulldogging steers, roping calves and trying to stay aboard bucking broncos and uncooperative bulls are challenges to test the mettle and physical ability of those who risk bruises and broken bones in their attempts to prove the superiority of man over beast. The Stetson hat, slim-cut jeans and cowboy boots are standard apparel for many of the state's non-city residents; and although pickup trucks and even motorbikes have taken over some of the chores, the horse is still cherished for both work and recreation.

Vermillion Plain Talk, *Tom Nelson photo*   Argus Leader

Black Hills, Badlands & Lakes Association

Black Hills, Badlands & Lakes Association

Black Hills, Badlands & Lakes Association

South Dakota Magazine

163

The coyote is South Dakota's state animal,
but it is also notoriously destructive of
young livestock. In the 1930s, aviator Clyde
Ice and hunting partners used a plane to
kill more than 300 of the predators when
lamb and calf losses were especially high.
South Dakota Magazine

Once headed for extinction, bison have made a strong comeback as large herds now inhabit Wind Cave National Park and Custer State Park. As part of good management practices, an annual buffalo roundup is held in the fall, and surplus animals are sold at auction. South Dakota Tourism

According to Indian legend, the Sioux Nation had its genesis after a great flood that inundated the whole world except for one high cliff. An eagle saved a maiden by taking her to the safe haven. Twins were born to the maiden, and the eagle was the father. Famed artist Oscar Howe illustrated the traditional story in one of his paintings titled "Origin of the Sioux." Oscar Howe Family collection, copyright by Adelheid Howe

Seven Council Fires

The conflict of cultures between European Caucasians and the Sioux Indians has persisted throughout the documented history of the land that became South Dakota. Ironically enough, both groups were immigrants into the region that they would eventually share in a spectrum of relationships, which ranged from close personal friendship among individuals to the extremes of bitter hostility and war. In between were varying shades of peaceful coexistence, aloof disregard for one another and, sadly enough, undeniable prejudices.

Through the years, broad-brush generalizations and thoughtless stereotyping have perpetuated much racial discord. And mutual misunderstanding of one another's motives, traditions, religions and values has added to the divisiveness. The fact remains, however, that settlers and Sioux were brought together fatefully on the same limited portion of the globe and each has added a special dimension to South Dakota's unique heritage.

Village dwellers—the Mound Builders, Mandans, Hidatsas and Arickaras— preceded the Sioux to the plainsland, but their influence on succeeding events was quite limited. On the other hand, the western migration of the tribes of the Seven Council Fires was to have a lasting effect on the territory to which their quest for buffalo led them.

Sioux has never been their preferred name, although its earlier Chippewa meaning of "snake" or "enemy" has been generally forgotten. Instead the term "Dakota" linked seven closely related tribes in an Alliance of Friends, with their differences being largely a matter of the three dialects they spoke. The Seven Council Fires included the Wahpetons, Sissetons, Mdewakantons and Wahpekutes, known collectively as Santees (Dakotas); the Yanktons and Yanktonnais (Nakotas); and the Tetons or Prairie People (Lakotas). The Tetons, in turn, consisted of seven subtribes: Oglala, Brule, Hunkpapa, Minneconjou, Blackfeet, Two Kettle and Sans Arc.

As the various bands gradually migrated from the woodlands of Minnesota to the open prairie, they established themselves in loosely defined regions: the Yanktons along the Missouri on both

Carl Bodmer, a 24-year-old Swiss artist, accompanied Prince Alexander Phillip Maximilian of Wied up the Missouri River in 1833 and drew many pictures of Plains Indians for the book Prince Maximilian eventually published. One of Bodmer's classic paintings was of Big Soldier, a Teton Sioux. Robinson Museum

sides of the James River, the Yanktonnais farther north in the James and Big Sioux valleys, the four Santee tribes in the vicinity of Big Stone Lake and the Tetons spreading out on the plains, deposing the Arickaras and eventually crossing the Missouri where the horses and rifles they acquired gave them greater hunting opportunities.

The free-spirited Indians had little knowledge of or interest in the European concept of land ownership, but when this system was imposed on them, they were caught up in a seemingly endless series of councils and treaty-signings, which, in time, would completely change their way of life. Many of their leaders were dressed in unfamiliar clothing and hauled off to Washington, D.C., for negotiations in which language differences, duplicity and "firewater" were factors to their disadvantage.

In 1858 the Yanktons were the first to

cede their lands, some 14 million acres in exchange for a small reservation, annuities for 50 years and other emoluments, including free use of the Red Pipestone Quarry for "so long as they shall desire." After that came a succession of pacts and federal laws which, in the end, relegated the Great Sioux Nation to the confines of seven reservations: Pine Ridge, Rosebud, Crow Creek, Lower Brule, Cheyenne River, Standing Rock and Lake Traverse (the latter being dissolved by subsequent legislation).

The complexities and subtle nuances of white-Indian relationships fill volumes; and, after a century of statehood, there were still lingering differences to be resolved. It should be recognized that the whites—in their respective time periods— were not always ill-intentioned as some writers seem to imply. The missionaries believed firmly that they were serving God and the Indians as well, while the proponents of assimilating and educating the tribespeople "in the ways of the white man" were not all devious and self-serving. There were social experiments and searches for solutions in each new generation—the "peace policy" of President Grant, the attempts at de-Indianization at the Carlisle Indian School and elsewhere, the Dawes Allotment Act of 1887 and the various other proposals. Each had an effect—some good, some bad—but the evolution, as it turned out, was destined to be a long, continuing process.

The interracial history of the state includes the Battle of Slim Buttes in 1876 and the Ghost Dance expectations, which led to the infamous massacre at Wounded Knee in 1890. Indian heroes have included Sitting Bull, Crazy Horse, Dr. Charles Eastman, Red Cloud, Blue Cloud and Billy Mills, the Olympic champion. U.S. Congressman Ben Reifel became the first Sioux to achieve such lofty office, while the fame of artist Oscar Howe grows year by year.

In the progression of time, reservations have seen the beginnings of colleges, newspapers, radio stations and state basketball champions. Meanwhile, the sharing of South Dakota goes on as Indians and non-Indians of tolerance and good will pursue a common dream of harmony and mutual respect.

Oscar Howe, known as the Indian artist laureate, was born on the Crow Creek Reservation in 1915. His vividly colored paintings in a unique geometric style preserve the heritage of his Sioux ancestors. Shown here (standing) with three of his students, he studied and taught at Dakota Wesleyan in Mitchell, served as art teacher at Pierre High School for 14 years and then was appointed artist-in-residence at the University of South Dakota, where he also earned his master's degree. His work has been exhibited both nationally and internationally, and for a number of years he designed the decorative panels of the Mitchell Corn Palace. He died in 1984. Friend of the Middle Border Museum

The dance, in various forms, has had religious, ceremonial and entertainment connotations for the Sioux Indians for centuries. Elders have encouraged younger generations to carry on traditional ways. Timber Lake and Area Historical Society, Frank Cundill photo, above; South Dakota Tourism, Paul Horsted photo, right

(Opposite page) "Eagle Dancer," a popular Oscar Howe painting, captures the rhythm and agility of a Sioux dancer. The extended arms of the dancer portray an eagle in flight, with head down in search of prey. Work by the South Dakota Indian artist is prized by collectors and grows more valuable with each passing year. Oscar Howe Family collection, copyright by Adelheid Howe

This Indian grave site near Highway 34 in northwest South Dakota is an indication that Christianity has become part of the Sioux heritage. Church leaders have learned that Native Americans—whom they once called heathens—have spiritual values and traditions that complement and enhance Catholic and Protestant traditions. South Dakota Magazine

One of the most meaningful symbols of the Sioux culture is the circle or hoop. Lame Deer said: "Our circle is timeless, flowing; it is new life emerging from death . . ."

This fundamental belief is celebrated in the traditional Indian hoop dance. South Dakota Tourism, Paul Horsted photo

This historic photo by I. B. Coleman includes the key participants in the negotiations that resulted in the cession of Yankton Sioux lands in 1858. Seated (left to right) were: Chief Strike-the-Ree, Zephier Rencontre and The Pretty Boy. Standing: Medicine Cow, Charles Picotte and Louis Dewitt. For his part in the dealings, Picotte, whose mother was a Yankton, received a 640-acre grant situated at the site of the territorial capital. Yankton County Historical Society

The Sioux did not have a written language but important happenings were sometimes preserved in pictographs on animal skins, which were called "winter counts." This one by a warrior named Lone Dog has been interpreted to cover the years from 1800 to 1871, beginning in the center. It depicts seven references to trade with whites, four epidemics of white man's diseases and 24 inter-tribal conflicts. Robinson Museum

Color and pageantry add to the excitement of later-day pow-wows. Modern dancers wear brightly colored costumes, while the earth-tone garb of traditionalists are reminiscent of what the Sioux wore a century ago. The American flag is an appropriate part of such ceremonies because many Sioux men have served with distinction in U.S. wars. South Dakota Tourism, Paul Horsted photo

This pictograph attributed to Sitting Bull showed him killing an Assiniboin warrior in his earlier years. He apparently made this and other paintings while he was in the custody of the U.S. Army following his return from Canada, where he learned to write well enough to sign his name. When he was with Buffalo Bill's Wild West Show, he sold autographs for a dollar apiece to augment his weekly salary of $50. Smithsonian Institution

This artist's sketch of an Indian encampment on Big Stone Lake dates back to the 1820s. Before the advent of photography, the drawings of Carl Bodmer, George Catlin and other less talented frontier visitors were the only graphic portrayals of Plains Indians available to curious Easterners and Europeans. R. B. Swanberg collection

The Sioux Indians were popular subjects of pioneer photographers Stanley J. Morrow, Frank Cundill, H. A. Perry, J. C. H. Grabill and others. Some individuals were identified, some were not, but at least the early-day cameras preserved authentic pictorial records of various tribespeople in the late 19th-century and early 20th century. Collections of Indian photographs are maintained in numerous repositories, including those of the South Dakota State Historical Society, the Center for Western Studies, the Buechel Memorial Lakota Museum, the W. H. Over Museum, the Douglas County Historical Society, Blue Cloud Abbey, the Timber Lake and Area Historical Society and others.

The blanket became part of Plains Indian dress through the course of dealing with white traders. Crow Dog (below), a Brule, and an unidentified Lakota woman at Pine Ridge appeared in typical blanket apparel. The Sioux were not weavers, so clothing, other than that with a natural fur or leather base, had to come from other sources. South Dakota State Historical Society, below; Clyde Goin collection, right

176

Photographer David F. Barry took this picture of Rain in the Face at the Standing Rock Reservation in 1886. A Lakota Hunkpapa, he was a member of the agency's Indian police force. South Dakota State Historical Society

A Catholic Indian mission school was built at Stephan south of Highmore on the Crow Creek Reservation in 1887. Six years later, these Sioux converts joined Father Fintan Wiederker on December 26, 1893, for a photograph following Christmas services the previous day. Blue Cloud Abbey

A typical 19th century Indian encampment was preserved for posterity in this vintage photograph. Before the passing of the buffalo and the signing of various treaties changed their lifestyle, the Sioux were a nomadic people with portable homes and no limitations of property ownership. Siouxland Heritage Museums

Indians were subjected to council after council in the continuing negotiations over land cessions, annuities and other matters. Tribal representatives were occasionally dressed in unfamiliar white man's clothing for trips to Washington, D.C., as were the delegates shown here (below) from the Cheyenne River Reservation in 1888. Other meetings and treaty-signing gatherings were held at various encampments, such as the one (left) where Chief Medicine Bear of the Yanktonnais stated his case before government officials. Smithsonian Institution, below; W. H. Over Museum, Stanley J. Morrow collection, left

This photograph of the Rosebud Indian Agency was taken in 1889, the year South Dakota's six permanent reservations were created. The so-called Messiah War was brewing at the time, and before the tragedy at Wounded Knee, soldiers dug rifle pits around the compound to protect it from possible attack. Nearby is the grave of Spotted Tail, the Brule chief, after whom the agency was originally named. South Dakota State Historical Society

The gradual meshing of cultures was evident in this photograph of Sisseton Indians of the Lake Traverse Reservation in 1886. Contrasting with native regalia and the traditional tepee were a military drum, a white man's buggy and an American flag. W. H. Over Museum, Stanley J. Morrow collection

Religious rituals, often involving smoking of the sacred pipe, were a fundamental part of Sioux tradition from ancient times. Medicine men were highly revered, and there was a spiritual foundation underlying the Indian lifestyle. Early Christian missionaries, in their zeal, often failed to recognize this fact as they competed in their efforts to convert the "heathen" natives. *South Dakota State Historical Society, left; Clyde Goin collection, below*

Totanka Yotanka (Sitting Bull) was a Hunkpapa medicine man and not a chief as he has often been mislabeled. His influence throughout the Sioux Nation was great, and it is said that a vision he had predicted the Indian victory at Little Big Horn. For a time he appeared in Buffalo Bill Cody's Wild West Show and, as the result of the publicity, became one of the most widely known, but often misunderstood, members of his race. *South Dakota State Historical Society*

Sitting Bull was shot to death on December 15, 1890, in his cabin on the Standing Rock Reservation. He was being arrested by a troop of Indian police because agency officials feared he would lead an uprising in the wake of the Ghost Dance movement. South Dakota State Historical Society

Indians killed during the Wounded Knee massacre on December 29, 1890, were commemorated by this monument at the site. The dead included Chief Big Foot, who presumably was leading his small band of Minneconjous to Pine Ridge to turn themselves in. He was suffering from pneumonia and riding in the back of a wagon when his party was intercepted by troopers of the 7th Cavalry, who were ordered to disarm the Indians. Yankton County Historical Society

After the massacre at Wounded Knee, Young Man Afraid of His Horses—chief of the Oglala Tetons—was instrumental in avoiding further confrontations. He was photographed at the Pine Ridge Agency in 1891. South Dakota State Historical Society

Dr. Charles A. Eastman was a Santee Sioux who became a college-trained physician. He later returned to South Dakota and in 1890 hurried from Pine Ridge to treat the survivors at Wounded Knee. He described the carnage he saw as "a severe ordeal for one who has so lately put all his faith in the Christian love and lofty ideals of the white man." South Dakota State Historical Society

Pioneer photographer Frank Cundill took a picture of Armstrong Four Bear taking a picture. A nationally known rodeo performer, Armstrong was the son of Chief Four Bear of the Two Kettles. Chief Four Bear had been a member of the legendary "Fool Soldiers" band that rescued the captive women and children of the Santee uprising in 1862. Timber Lake and Area Historical Society, Frank Cundill photo

Armstrong Four Bear gained fame as a bronc rider and showman, performing at rodeos and Wild West shows throughout the country. The Sioux cowboy from the Cheyenne River Reservation was also a trick rope artist. Timber Lake and Area Historical Society, Frank Cundill photo

183

The tepee was a practical, movable dwelling when the Sioux tribes were nomadic. On the reservations, however, more permanent homes were built, although they usually took the form of crude log huts that provided little more than basic protection from the elements. Clyde Goin collection

Travel by harnessed horse and wagon instead of by pony and travois (center) was another major adjustment the Indians had to make. Instead of moving from hunt to hunt, they journeyed across dusty prairie trails from various settlements to get their ration allotments. This caravan (right) was en route to the Cheyenne River Agency. South Dakota State Historical Society

The various treaties provided government annuities to the Sioux, including a periodic issue of beef, which came on the hoof. In some cases the cattle were turned loose and shot from horseback in a symbolic renewal of a buffalo hunt. Indians did their own slaughtering on the reservations, and the occasions were usually a time for tribal gatherings and celebrations. *South Dakota State Historical Society*

The sweat lodge has both health and religious implications among the Sioux. This photo was taken in 1898 at the Cut Meat Camp School on the Rosebud Reservation. *South Dakota State Historical Society*

Frank Cundill, who homesteaded nine miles south of Firesteel in 1911, left a legacy of historic photographs, many of which he took prior to World War I. His pictorial record of life on the Standing Rock and Cheyenne River reservations has proved especially valuable as his camera preserved for future generations the tradi- tions, dress, dwellings and other elements of Sioux heritage still evident at the time in Dewey, Ziebach and Corson counties. The rancher-photographer was a member of the South Dakota Board of Regents (1937-55) and the State Fish and Game Commission (1931-37). He died in 1965. Timber Lake and Area Historical Society

CUNDILL

CUNDILL HONYOCKER PHOTO

Making Moccasins

© PC

INDIAN POLICE

CUNDILL PHOTO.

SERIES NO. 4
F. CUNDILL

CUNDILL MONTOCKER PHOTO

Two of a kind   ©F.C.

*Variations in Indian dress are well shown
in this unusual group photograph. The
Sioux combined trade beads, bells and other
imported doodads with such traditional
natural materials as eagle feathers, porcu-
pine quills and fringed leather in the creation of their colorful ceremonial wear.
Clyde Goin collection*

Minneconjou elders from the Cherry Creek area met with Governor Robert S. Vessey (second row center) who was the state's chief executive from 1909 through 1913. Unending differences over treaty provisions continued to go unresolved after more than a century of negotiations. South Dakota State Historical Society

In the continuing—and often competitive—effort to Christianize the Sioux, numerous missions, churches and schools were established by the various denominations. This Congregational Church at Green Grass on the Cheyenne River Reservation had both white and Indian parishioners. Timber Lake and Area Historical Society, Frank Cundill photo

At the Yankton Agency both the Congregationalists (above) and the Episcopalians (right) built substantial structures for their missions. W. H. Over Museum, Stanley J. Morrow collection

194

In 1927 an order known as Priests of the Sacred Heart purchased the vacated buildings of Columbus College, which had moved from Chamberlain to Sioux Falls. St. Joseph's Indian School was established on the same grounds where the U.S. government had operated a boarding school for Sioux youngsters many years earlier. The young boy, pictured with a toy top and headdress, symbolized the mixing of cultures. St. Joseph's Indian School

Calf-branding at the Cherry Creek Day School on the Cheyenne River Reservation was both a ranching necessity and an educational experience for Indian youngsters. Many sons and grandsons of earlier buffalo hunters adapted to the role of the working cowboy. Clyde Goin collection

At the Oglala Boarding School on the Pine Ridge Reservation, Lakota youngsters were trained as seamstresses, printers, bakers, harness-makers and other occupations. The concepts of assimilation and deculturiza-tion were accepted by some and rejected by others in the continuing effort to resolve the differences between Indians and non-Indians. *South Dakota State Historical Society*

President Calvin Coolidge, who established his Summer White House in Custer State Park in 1927, was made an honorary chief of the Sioux Indians and given the name Chief Leading Eagle. Presenting the headdress was Rosebud Yellow Robe. South Dakota State Historical Society

At Cherry Creek, Lazy White Bull, a nephew of Sitting Bull, posed on two different occasions with the obvious evidence of changing conditions on the reservation. The wagon had replaced the travois, and then the automobile came along to erode further the traditional ways. Clyde Goin collection

In 1930, Sacred Heart Church was erected at Wounded Knee, 40 years after the infamous massacre. Four decades later—in 1973—it was burned down as the result of a demonstration led by the American Indian Movement, which became known as Wounded Knee II. The cemetery and part of the massacre site was later donated to the Oglala tribe by officials of the church that owned the land. *South Dakota State Historical Society*

Indian ball teams have been prominent in South Dakota athletic history. Reservation schools have produced state basketball champions and outstanding track stars. The greatest was Billy Mills from Pine Ridge, who won the gold medal for the United States in the 10,000 meter run in the 1964 Olympics. *Buechel Memorial Lakota Museum, St. Francis Indian Mission*

Before his death in 1973, Ben Black Elk—an Oglala Sioux—was reputedly the most photographed Indian of all time. During the peak of the tourist season, he posed for several thousand pictures daily at the Shrine to Democracy. He became known as the "fifth face of Mount Rushmore." He was the son of the famed medicine man and warrior who was present at Little Big Horn, Wounded Knee and the killing of Crazy Horse at Fort Robinson, Neb. He was the subject of poet John G. Neihardt's noted book, "Black Elk Speaks." Black Hills, Badlands & Lakes Association, left; South Dakota State Historical Society, above

199

In 1986, Joe Flying Boy, a Teton medicine man, conducted a Memorial Day service for Sioux warrior dead at Sitting Bull's grave near Mobridge. The ceremony was sponsored by the Standing Rock Reservation and Indian members of the American Legion and Veterans of Foreign Wars. Sculptor Korczak Ziolkowski created the bust of the famed Hunkpapa medicine man. Mobridge Tribune, *Larry Atkinson photo*

One of South Dakota's most bizarre stories could be titled "The Night They Stole Sitting Bull." The Hunkpapa medicine man had been buried at Fort Yates, N.D., but there was a continuing effort to have his remains returned to the Grand River country. When normal methods failed to achieve results, a group of South Dakotans—with the approval of Sitting Bull's relatives—made a night-time raid on the cemetery, exhumed the bones of the famous Sioux leader, rushed back across the border and quickly reinterred them in a grave on the west side of the Missouri near Mobridge. To make sure that this would be Sitting Bull's final resting place, the conspirators poured 20 tons of concrete over the steel vault containing his casket. A point of controversy was to continue, however. Some North Dakotans insisted that the raiders got the wrong bones. Mobridge Tribune

William Fuller, a carpenter at Crow Creek Agency in 1893, painted this idyllic version of reservation life. Included within the picture are (standing, from left): the artist himself; Mark Wells, an interpreter; and Talking Crow, head of the Indian police. Seated are Chief White Ghost and Chief Bull Ghost. Robinson Museum

Majestic, Mystical Black Hills

It has been said that the Black Hills of South Dakota are big enough to be majestic, but—unlike the Rockies—small enough to be comprehensible.

So named because of the ebon hue created by thick stands of various coniferous trees on their ridges and in their ravines, they are the state's principal lure for tourists who come to enjoy the natural wonders and a wide variety of man-made attractions, which range from reptile gardens and concrete dinosaurs to the incomparable masterpiece of Gutzon Borglum at Mount Rushmore.

It is difficult, if not impossible, to describe the Black Hills in capsule form. First, there is the 1,250,000-acre Black Hills National Forest that encompasses much of the region. Adjacent to or surrounded by the forest are Custer State Park, Wind Cave National Park, Mount Rushmore National Memorial and Jewel Cave National Monument.

On the periphery—from the Belle Fourche Reservoir in the north to the Angostura Reservoir in the south—are geographic features that bear little resemblance to the rest of South Dakota. Northeast of Sturgis, Bear Butte rises incongruously from the plains to an elevation of 4,422 feet. Within the national forest, Harney Peak towers almost three thousand feet higher, the tallest mountain in the United States east of the Rockies.

Unfortunately, the Hills were once considered to be just part of the Great American Desert when they were included in the Sioux Reserve granted to the Indians by the Fort Laramie Treaty of

Sioux Indians called these mountains Paha Sapa *(black hills) because the forests of pine and spruce appear dark from a distance. They also called them* O'onakezin, *which means "place of shelter," and* Wamakaognaka E'cante, *meaning "the heart of everything that is." South Dakota Tourism, Paul Horsted*

1868. There were no crystal balls available to predict future events that would make mockery of the treaty provisions and generate a controversy that, more than a century later, would continue unresolved.

Article 2 of the Laramie document was interpreted to allow an exploratory expedition led by Lt. Col. George Armstrong Custer and his 7th Cavalry Regiment into the Region in 1874. In itself this would have been but minor trespass, but in the process the expedition's miners— Horatio Nelson Ross and William T. McKay—discovered gold in French Creek near the present city of Custer.

When the news was finally circulated, there were not soldiers enough to stem the tide of prospectors rushing in for the riches. They congregated in the greatest numbers in and around Deadwood Gulch where the Days of '76 would thereafter be annually remembered. Hay Town, which was renamed Rapid City, got its start as a supply point. At Lead, various claims were eventually combined to create the giant Homestake Mining Company of George Hearst and partners.

There was no turning back. By the time the gold fever had subsided, permanent settlement of the Black Hills was an accomplished reality, treaty or not. During the gold rush and its aftermath, the region was supplied entirely by freight wagons on long hauls from Bismarck; Pierre; Chadron, Nebraska; and other terminals. Finally, in 1885, the Fremont, Elkhorn and Missouri Valley Railroad extended its track to Buffalo Gap and in the following year to Rapid City. From then on the dependency on horses, mules and oxen was past. Unlike eastern Dakota, where the railroads had spurred the homesteading boom, in the Hills the first track was laid to take advantage of what had already occurred.

For almost 18 years after South Dakota entered the Union, the Black Hills region was virtually isolated from the rest of the state because of the lack of east-west transportation. Not until rail connections were made from Pierre and Chamberlain in 1907 did the state become a truly cohesive unit.

While forest and mineral wealth provided a substantial economic base, the

In 1937 sculptor Gutzon Borglum draped an American flag over Abraham Lincoln's granite likeness on Mount Rushmore, then removed it during a ceremonial unveiling. The National Park Service used Old Glory again in 1987 as a backdrop for an anniversary of the historic occasion in Rushmore history. South Dakota Tourism, Paul Horsted photo

idea of the Black Hills as a vacationland began to develop. Hot Springs had already begun attracting visitors as a health spa before the advent of the automobile. A national spotlight was focused on the region in 1927 when President Calvin Coolidge selected the State Game Lodge in Custer State Park as his Summer White House, and thereafter tourism became a leading industry.

Despite the many natural attractions in the Hills, it remained for the inspired work of an artist to provide the *piece de resistance*. In 1927 sculptor Gutzon Borglum began the monstrous task of chipping away at Mount Rushmore to create his matchless Shrine to Democracy. Altogether some 450,000 tons of rock fell to hammer, chisel and blasting powder before the faces of George Washington, Thomas Jefferson, Theodore Roosevelt and Abraham Lincoln were

completed for dedication on July 2, 1939, as the highlight of South Dakota's 50th year of statehood.

Elsewhere in the Hills, the legends of such characters as Calamity Jane, Wild Bill Hickok, Henry Weston "Preacher" Smith and Poker Alice Tubbs live on. At Spearfish, in sharp contrast, the renowned Passion Play has continued a religious tradition since 1939. Mysteries of the past have been revealed at the Mammoth Site near Hot Springs, while the family of the late Korczak Ziolkowski pursues his dream of a 563-foot sculpture at Crazy Horse Mountain. Spearfish Canyon, the granite spires of the Needles and the pigtails, switchbacks and tunnels of the unusual Iron Mountain Road all add to the magnetic charm of *Paha Sapa*, the alter ego of South Dakota's plainsland, while enhancing the state's claim as the Land of Infinite Variety.

Sure-footed mountain goats are often sighted on Mount Rushmore. The goats are not native to South Dakota. Six were brought from Alberta, Canada, in 1924 by the State Game, Fish and Parks Depart-

ment, and by the 1980s their numbers were estimated at 120. They stay close to the Harney Peak area and have not spread to other parts of the Hills. National Park Service

The Needles, rugged granite pinnacles and knobs that rise to an elevation of 7,166 feet, have great attractions for climbers, geologists and photographers. The Needles Highway, the inspiration of Peter Norbeck, takes visitors through the natural sculptures, which represent an inch of erosion for every 40 thousand years. South Dakota Tourism, Mark Kayser

The late Badger Clark, South Dakota's best-loved poet, said more youthful mountain ranges "show wide expanses of nudity, in the fashion of young people on the beach; but the Hills, in their green and vigorous old age, have become conservative and are clothed from neck to ankle—in ponderosa pine." South Dakota Tourism, Paul Horsted photo

Pactola Reservoir, nestled in a valley thick with ponderosa pine, is a favorite playground of natives and vacationers. Pactola was once a booming gold camp that got its name from the Pactolus River of ancient Lydia in Asia Minor, a stream noted for its golden sands. South Dakota Tourism

Credit for discovering Wind Cave in 1881 goes to Thomas Bingham who supposedly was terrified when a blast of subterranean air blew his hat off while he was deer hunting in Custer County. Indians, of course, knew of the strange phenomenon long before that. More than 34 miles of tunnels have been explored in the cave, which was designated a National Park in 1903. The early-day entrance facilities (below) have since been replaced. South Dakota State Historical Society, below; South Dakota Tourism, Paul Horsted photo, right

Entrance to Wind Cave, S.D.

Some of the largest and longest caves in the United States have been discovered under the Black Hills. They feature cavernous rooms, unique stalagmites and stalactites, sparkling crystals and other formations. Jewel Cave, now a National Monument, is considered the fourth longest in the world, with at least 69 miles of explored tunnels. *South Dakota Tourism*

Benedictine monks prepared for a holiday service in Bethlehem Cave north of Rapid City, one of numerous subterranean attractions for tourists, spelunkers and speleologists. Formerly known as Crystal Cave, it was discovered in 1890. *South Dakota Tourism*

Construction crews were leveling a site for a housing project at Hot Springs in 1974 when they unearthed large bones and teeth. The accidental archaeological find, now called the Mammoth Site, is one of the largest discoveries of prehistoric elephantine remains in the world. Scientists believe the animals died some 26,000 years ago when they became trapped in a spring-fed pond. *South Dakota Tourism, Paul Horsted photo*

The famed 7th Cavalry Regiment commanded by the colorful and controversial George Armstrong Custer (right) left an indelible mark on South Dakota history. In 1873 the unit first arrived at Yankton where Custer almost died of pneumonia in an April blizzard. A year later, the flamboyant lieutenant colonel (who had been a brevet general in the Civil War) led his men on the expedition into the Black Hills (center). While the troops were there, gold was discovered. (W. H. Illingworth photographed his officers and scientific corps in camp at Box Elder Creek, bottom.) Ironically, the treaty-breaking gold rush of '76 was taking place while Custer and many of his troopers were being annihilated at Little Big Horn. In 1890 a reconstituted 7th Cavalry force participated in the massacre at Wounded Knee, which some historians say was partly influenced by a revenge motive against the Indians. South Dakota State Historical Society

George Custer cut a colorful trail as he crisscrossed the Territory of Dakota. Photographer William H. Illingworth captured this pose of the flamboyant military leader after he killed a grizzly bear in the southern Black Hills during the expedition of 1874. South Dakota State Historical Society

The discovery of gold in the Black Hills by the Custer expedition generated quick and widespread interest. The first group of "sooners" attempting to thwart the provisions of the Laramie Treaty of 1868 was the Gordon party from Sioux City, Iowa, which built a pine log stockade near Custer in late 1874. The army evicted the trespassers, who included Annie D. Tallent, the first white woman in the Black Hills. Later, the government simply gave up trying to stem the tide of prospectors. Wall Drug Store collection

The demand for logs and lumber during the gold rush era was intense. For many disappointed prospectors, providing construction materials was more profitable than mining. Sawmills, like the ones pictured here, did a rushing business. Unfortunately, the early lumberjacks had little regard for conservation, and soon the hills and gulches were scarred and barren. *Wall Drug Store collection*

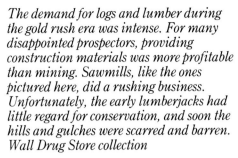

It was one thing to find the gold and another to protect it, which was why this miner apparently sat on guard at his tent near Deadwood. The picture might have been "staged" by photographer Stanley J. Morrow, who made an occasional practice of contriving a shot to depict an activity or an event he considered important enough to preserve on film. *W. H. Over Museum, Stanley J. Morrow collection*

Miners' shacks in Bear Gulch indicate that all was not glamorous in the pursuit of gold. Living conditions were minimal at best, and it took lots of stoop labor and shovel work to produce a day's wages. South Dakota State Historical Society

The log town of Gayville in Deadwood Gulch was named for brothers Albert and William Gay on whose claims it was platted in 1876. According to an early issue of The Black Hills Pioneer, *Gayville soon had some 250 houses and more than 30 business establishments, but after ten years of feverish activity, the claims began to play out and miners moved on to new diggings. Black Hills, Badlands & Lakes Association*

The Black Hills gold rush attracted Chinese miners whose frugality and meticulousness permitted them to make a living from tailings and panning sites passed up by white prospectors. They established their own community between Elizabethtown and Deadwood and were the victims of considerable prejudice. Pictured here is the winning firefighting team of an all-Chinese hose race held at Deadwood's 1888 Fourth of July celebration. South Dakota State Historical Society

Lead City (later Lead, pronounced Leed) was first known as Washington when it was founded in 1876. It was renamed when it was combined with the adjoining mining camp of Golden. The name is derived from its location over a rich vein or "lead" of gold-bearing quartz, which made it the site of the famous Homestake Mine. Wall Drug Store collection

Charles Collins, shown at the door of the shack in which he published the Black Hills Champion, *was a maverick Irishman who instigated the first expedition of "sooners" to flaunt the terms of the Fort Laramie treaty. Later he tried to establish an Irish colony at Brule City, south of present-day Chamberlain, where he hoped to raise an army to drive the hated British out of Canada. This sketch appeared in* Frank Leslie's Illustrated Weekly *of New York. Western Historical Research Center, University of Wyoming*

Newspapers that survived the hand-press era installed steam-driven platens and cylinders. This is the pressroom of the Deadwood Pioneer-Times, *with the printers and staff members obviously dressed for the photographic occasion. South Dakota Press Association*

Mormon prospectors erected a meeting house in Deadwood during the early days of the gold rush. It was in sharp contrast to the saloons and gaming parlors that sprang up in the gulch, where literally thousands of young men congregated in search of excitement and sudden wealth. W. H. Over Museum, Stanley J. Morrow collection

W. R. Stebbins, Samuel N. Wood and
M. E. Post established the first bank in
Deadwood in 1877 to serve the area's
miners. A year later it was chartered as the
First National Bank of Deadwood. Much
of its early business involved the handling
of gold dust and nuggets. After several
mergers and changes of ownership, it eventually evolved into the Deadwood branch of
Norwest Banks.

Law enforcement during territorial days and the early years of statehood included several hangings. The last legal use of the gallows in Meade County occurred in 1902 when Ernest Loves War was executed at Sturgis for the axe-gunshot murders of two ranchers from Red Owl. The state's most famous hanging was at Yankton in 1877 when Jack McCall was given the noose for the shooting of Wild Bill Hickok. Wall Drug Store collection

Almost all the "facts" about Martha Jane Canary—better known as Calamity Jane—are open to question. Different writers list her birthplace as Iowa, Illinois, Missouri and Montana, and at varying dates. She has been described as a bullwhacker, a military scout, an angel of mercy (for treating smallpox victims), a woman of ill repute and the paramour of Wild Bill Hickok. One thing is for certain: she was truly an extraordinary character in Black Hills history. Montana Historical Society, above; Yankton Historical Society, right

Calamity Jane died in 1903 and is buried in Deadwood's Mt. Moriah cemetery. Her grave is beside that of Wild Bill Hickok, who, legend has it, was once her sweetheart. Clyde Goin collection

Cavalry troopers at Fort Meade near Sturgis trained their mounts to lie flat on the ground to be used as living barriers against bullets and arrows, if needed. Fort Meade was first garrisoned in 1878 and was named for General George G. Meade, who commanded Union forces at the battle of Gettysburg. Friends of the Middle Border Museum

Members of the South Dakota Press Association, shown here near Deadwood, were hosted by Pierre on a cross-country tour from the Missouri to the Black Hills in 1890. It was part of the campaign by the city to retain its designation as the state's capital. The publishers—who in those days had free passes on all the railroads—used them to travel through Nebraska to Sioux City and back to their homes. South Dakota Press Association

As color played out in the streams, miners with workable claims went underground for gold-bearing ore. Crude, hand-pushed trams operating on wooden rails were the first attempts at mechanization. Wall Drug Store collection

Theodore Reder made his fortune in the lumber business during and after the Black Hills gold rush, but in 1882 he conceived a grandiose plan for damming Sunday Gulch, creating a lake and building a fine resort hotel. He and his brother Charles acquired the land in 1891 and proceeded to construct a dam 40 feet wide and 33 feet high to form beautiful Sylvan Lake. Theodore's wife Elizabeth drew the plans for the three-story, 66-room hotel and pagoda, which were completed in 1895. The resort continued as a popular lodging destination for tourists and honeymooners until it was destroyed by fire in 1936. Center for Western Studies

Generally, settlers followed the railroads into the new frontiers of Dakota Territory. The Black Hills region was an exception. Mining camps sprang up overnight as loggers, saloon-keepers, gamblers and gunfighters flocked to the rough new towns. It was 1886 before the first railroad reached Rapid City. Two years later the narrow-gauge Deadwood Central began operating in the high country, as gangs of construction workers completed the road-beds of the various lines. Wall Drug Store collection

In 1885 the Fremont, Elkhorn and Missouri Valley Railroad entered the Black Hills region at Buffalo Gap, an appropriate name for the pass through which large herds of bison traveled in their seasonal wanderings. At the celebration marking the railroad's arrival, the ceremonies included the symbolic driving of a tin spike, and soon after a 4½-ton specimen of tin ore was hauled to the Buffalo Gap station for shipment to the East for analysis. This temporary bank office was indicative of the new town's hopes for the future as a key railroad terminus. The optimism faded when the tracks were extended to Rapid City and beyond. South Dakota State Historical Society

Ox-drawn freight wagons churned up the Main Street of Sturgis in 1886. The town was platted eight years earlier, and there is a lingering question about whether it was named for Major Samuel D. Sturgis who commanded troops at Fort Meade at the time or for his son, Lieutenant J. G. Sturgis, who was killed at Little Big Horn. Wall Drug Store collection

The gold stamp mills of Terraville, located in Bobtail Gulch between Central City and Lead, were photographed in 1888 by J. C. H. Grabill, whose camera recorded many important scenes and developments of South Dakota's past. Wall Drug Store collection

222

In 1889, high water in Gold Run Creek turned the Deadwood Central's narrow-gauge track into a roller coaster. Electric trolleys eventually replaced steam trains for interurban passenger service in the Lead-Deadwood area. *South Dakota State Historical Society*

The movement of supplies to the various mining districts was a continuing challenge because of weather and terrain. This eight-mule team was photographed at Gold Run Gulch in 1889 enroute to the Homestake mines and mills. *Wall Drug Store collection*

One of many projects of Black Hills entrepreneur Frederick Taft Evans, his famous "Plunge" in Hot Springs was first enclosed in 1890. It is shown under construction and as it was when completed. Its well-advertised curative powers soon attracted bathers from afar; and, although the physical facilities were later modernized, it was still a popular warm water pool after 100 years of statehood. South Dakota State Historical Society

Fred Evans was a logger, horse wrangler, bank organizer, railroad promoter and builder of street railways, hotels and health spas. However, the source of his wealth came from the freighting business. The Evans Transportation Company existed for a dozen years after the discovery of gold in the Black Hills and hauled some 12 million pounds of freight by mule and ox-drawn wagon trains. Evans died in 1902 at the age of 67 after devoting his later years to the development of Hot Springs. Wall Drug Store collection

An Evans tallyho coach brought visitors to the healing and invigorating waters of Hot Springs in 1889. Two years later two railroad lines entered the resort town, which by then was gaining a national reputation. South Dakota State Historical Society

Hot Springs is noted for its historic buildings made of locally quarried sandstone. Thousands of visitors came to the Fall River city in the 1890s and early 1900s to seek cures in the warm mineral-water springs. Most stayed at the Evans Hotel (upper right), which was typical of the architecture. The Fremont, Elkhorn and Missouri River Valley train brought members of the National Association of Railway Surgeons to a convention in 1893. The Hot Springs depot was known as "the smallest Union Station in the world." South Dakota State Historical Society

The Hot Springs Sanatorium boasted miraculous healing powers. It gained fame when 30 invalid veterans of the Civil War were sent there from the Soldiers' Home at Leavenworth, Kansas, and all but two were reported entirely cured. The South Dakota State Veterans' Home was the first major sandstone building to be completed in Hot Springs in 1890. Center for Western Studies, Bessie Pettigrew collection

Spearfish, in the northern Black Hills, in later years became noted for its annual Passion Play featuring Josef Meier in the role of Christ. The historic but controversial Thoen Stone was found at Lookout Mountain near the town. A territorial teachers' school—Spearfish Normal—was authorized by the legislature in 1883. It later evolved into Black Hills State College. Clyde Goin collection

One of South Dakota's most scenic areas is the canyon formed by Spearfish Creek as it flows northward in Lawrence County from Cheyenne Crossing to the town of Spearfish, eventually emptying into the Redwater River. Roughlock Falls on Little Spearfish Creek remains a picturesque attraction, but the spectacular Spearfish Falls on the main stream was long ago diverted into an unsightly flume by the Homestake Mining Company. Clyde Goin collection

The American bison—popularly known as the buffalo—was saved from extinction by the efforts of James "Scotty" Philip and others who developed private herds. Hundreds of thousands of the majestic beasts once roamed the South Dakota plains and were literally the "supermarket" for Sioux Indians, providing food, clothing, shelter and utensils. Clyde Goin collection

In 1929, while prospecting in the stream from which his name was derived, Potato Creek Johnny Perrett found one of the largest gold nuggets in Black Hills history. He later sold the 7½-ounce prize for $250. He was a popular attraction at Deadwood's "Days of '76" before his death in 1942 at the age of 77. South Dakota State Historical Society

West-river hotels showed considerable improvement between 1907 when the tar-papered Granger Hotel welcomed guests at Stamford in Jackson County and 1928 when the classic Alex Johnson was completed in Rapid City. Photographed as it was in 1930, the old hotel—known for its elegant charm—has hosted hundreds of celebrities, including presidents of the United States. South Dakota State Historical Society

When the Dirty Thirties brought economic woes to the state, many South Dakotans found employment in various New Deal programs. A few of the more independent citizens turned to the tiny streams of the Black Hills with gold pans and sluicing equipment to try to eke out a few dollars a day. Clyde Goin collection

The Works Progress Administration, a New Deal program, built roads, bridges and even dinosaurs during the depression. Although construction of the concrete creatures may have seemed odd to the men who built them on government time, the pay-off has come in the delight of thousands of youngsters who have visited Rapid City's Dinosaur Park through the years, Clyde Goin collection, right; Black Hills, Badlands & Lakes Association, below

Long before the age of astronauts, Captains Orvil A. Anderson, pilot of Explorer II, and Albert W. Stevens, a scientist, wore football helmets to protect themselves in case of a rough landing. Fortunately, the balloon sailed through the Dakota sky for eight hours and landed uneventfully near White Lake. The total land distance traveled was about 200 miles. National Geographic Society

A world record-setting high altitude balloon flight was launched from the Stratosphere Bowl near Rapid City on November 11, 1935. Sponsored by the National Geographic Society and the U.S. Army Air Corps, the two-man crew of Explorer II soared to an altitude of 72,395 feet, more than 13 miles above the earth. National Geographic Society

Gutzon Borglum was lured to the challenge of Mount Rushmore by Doane Robinson, the state historian who conceived the idea of carving a giant Old West epic scene into one of the peaks of the Black Hills. Borglum (shown here giving detailed instructions as he did throughout the project) was feuding with the sponsors of a Confederate memorial he was creating at Stone Mountain in Georgia when the South Dakota proposal was presented to him. He finally agreed to pursue Robinson's idea of a massive sculpture at Rushmore, but he rejected the western theme in favor of a concept more national in scope. The four presidents were the result. Clyde Goin collection

When President Calvin Coolidge officially launched the gargantuan project at Mount Rushmore on August 10, 1927, he said: "We have come here to dedicate a cornerstone that was laid by the hand of the Almighty." He then presented ceremonial drill bits to Gutzon Borglum, sitting bald and hatless on the center of the platform. National Park Service

Working from detailed sketches and scale models by the artist, a select crew—including Borglum himself—began the almost superhuman task of blasting and chipping out the face of George Washington. The 6,040-foot mountain was named in a somewhat flippant manner after Charles E. Rushmore, a young New York attorney who was on a business visit to mining interests in the Black Hills when he casually asked the name of the impressive granite promontory. Supposedly his guide said: "Never had any, but it has now. We'll call the damned thing Rushmore." *South Dakota State Historical Society*

Work on the monumental task took not only talent but derring-do. The enormity of the sculpture is evident in the comparative sizes of the men and the nose of George Washington. Because of the touch-and-go financing and the economic conditions of the time, a few skilled craftsmen on the job received a dollar an hour, while drillers and other workers received half that amount for their risky assignments. *Clyde Goin collection*

Even before the Shrine to Democracy was completed, its magnetic attraction for tourists was evident. Since the early 1940s, literally millions of visitors have made the pilgrimage to Mount Rushmore, including many foreigners who come to South Dakota expressly "to see the faces." South Dakota State Historical Society

As the work progressed in the midst of the Great Depression, raising money for the venture was a constantly nagging challenge. A $5,000 donation from Charles

Rushmore, after whom the mountain had been named, helped get Borglum started. Eventually the federal government participated after much political haggling, while

South Dakota school children contributed pennies, nickels and dimes to the effort. Clyde Goin collection

Gutzon Borglum, an Idaho-born sculptor with a sense for the epic creation, explained progress on his Mount Rushmore masterpiece to President Franklin D. Roosevelt and Governor Tom Berry during Roosevelt's visit to the state in 1936. Borglum told the president that his carving would be comparable to the building of the Great Pyramids of Egypt and he called on the chief executive "to dedicate this memorial as a shrine to democracy." Borglum died unexpectedly in 1941 before the work was completed, but his monumental legacy and the title he ascribed to it were to live on for uncounted generations. Black Hills, Badlands & Lakes Association

Despite skeptics, government bureaucracy, limited funds and unexpected faults in the granite of Mount Rushmore, the magnificent Shrine to Democracy neared completion after more than a dozen years of intensified labor. A Hall of Records in the mountain behind the heads was never finished. There was still work to be done following the official dedication on July 2, 1939, and the unexpected death of the 74-year-old sculptor in 1941. It fell to Borglum's son, Lincoln, to add the finishing touches to his masterpiece. South Dakota State Historical Society

Bear Butte in Meade County—standing detached from the Black Hills at an elevation of 4,422 feet—provided geographic reference for early explorers and had religious significance for the Plains Indians, including the Mandans, the Cheyennes and the Sioux. Various legends are attributed to it. South Dakota Tourism

The Black Hills region is dotted with ramshackle reminders of past glories. The superintendent's house at Rochford's Standby Gold Mine is a typical, ghostly example. Clyde Goin collection

In the fur-trade era, beavers were highly prized among the animals that lured trappers to the upper Missouri. In later years, state trappers had to capture them alive to relocate them when their dams caused problems in Black Hills streams. *South Dakota Game, Fish and Parks Department*

In addition to a university and an agricultural college, territorial and state legislatures authorized five other institutions of higher learning. The School of Mines at Rapid City (shown as it appeared in the 1930s) was established in 1885. Eastern Normal School—oldest of four teachers' colleges—was founded in 1881 at Madison, Spearfish in 1883, Southern at Springfield in 1897 (although it had been authorized 16 years earlier) and Northern at Aberdeen in 1902. Various name and mission changes occurred through the years, and in 1983, Southern was converted into a minimum security prison. *Clyde Goin collection*

Iowa-born Charles Badger Clark, Jr. was the son of a Methodist minister, who homesteaded in Aurora County in 1883 when his youngest son was only four months old. The boy—who thereafter was known only by his middle name—was educated at Deadwood High School and Dakota Wesleyan before launching his career as a poet and lecturer. He never married and lived a Spartan existence in a Black Hills cabin he called the "Badger Hole" (location). The South Dakota legislature officially designated him as the state's first poet laureate in 1937. He died 20 years later and is buried at Hot Springs. His most famous poem he titled "A Cowboy's Prayer." It was reprinted so often without his byline that he sometimes referred to himself as "Mr. Anonymous." South Dakota State Historical Society

The plaque text reads:

WHEN THE COURSE OF HISTORY HAS BEEN TOLD
LET THESE TRUTHS HERE CARVED BE KNOWN
CONSCIENCE DICTATES CIVILIZATIONS LIVE
AND DUTY OURS TO PLACE BEFORE THE WORLD,
A CHRONICLE WHICH WILL LONG ENDURE.
FOR LIKE ALL THINGS UNDER US AND BEYOND
INEVITABLY WE MUST PASS INTO OBLIVION.

THIS LAND OF REFUGE TO THE STRANGER
WAS OURS FOR COUNTLESS EONS BEFORE:
CIVILIZATIONS MAJESTIC AND MIGHTY.
OUR GIFTS WERE MANY WHICH WE SHARED
AND GRATITUDE FOR THEM WAS KNOWN,
BUT LATER GIVEN MY OPPRESSED OWN
WERE MURDER RAPE AND SANGUINE WAR.

LOOKING FROM WHENCE INVADERS CAME,
GREEDY USURPERS OF OUR HERITAGE
FOR US THE PAST IS IN OUR HEARTS.
THE FUTURE NEVER TO BE FULFILLED
TO YOU I GIVE THIS GRANITE EPIC
FOR YOUR DESCENDANTS TO ALWAYS KNOW—
MY LANDS ARE WHERE MY DEAD LIE BURIED.

KORCZAK ZIOLKOWSKI

Colonel Caleb Carleton, the post commander at Fort Meade in 1892, ordered "The Star Spangled Banner" to be played at all retreats, parades and concerts because he and his wife were concerned that the United States had no national anthem. In time, the practice was picked up elsewhere until 1931, when Congress officially adopted the song. Governor Richard F. Kneip (at left) dedicated the plaque memorializing Colonel Carlton's contribution. Bob Lee photo

Korczak Ziolkowski believed the Rushmore Monument immortalized one part of American life but ignored another—the role of the American Indian. In 1947 he came to Thunderhead Mountain near Custer and began shaping his gargantuan monument to the Sioux war hero, Crazy Horse. Before his death in 1982, Korczak posed before a model of the image he planned to mold into the 6,700-foot mountain behind him. His wife, Ruth, and their ten children have dedicated themselves to completing the immense sculpture, which will be 641 feet long and 563 feet high, following three books full of drawings and instructions Korczak left them. South Dakota Tourism

Each year, tens of thousands of motor-cyclists gather for a rollicking rally at Sturgis in Meade County. They engage in competitive events, camaraderie, swapping, selling and occasional devilment. Bikers then spread out to see the other sights of the Black Hills. Black Hills, Badlands & Lakes Association, below; South Dakota State Historical Society, right

The mammoth Homestake Mining Company at Lead grew from the small claims of Fred and Moses Manuel, which Californian George Hearst and partners bought for $70,000 in 1877. With subsequent additions, it became one of the world's richest gold mine properties of all time. Homestake Mining Company

Bridal Veil Falls—so named because of the filmy flow of water over the rocks in Spearfish Canyon—provided a unique practice opportunity for mountain climbers during a winter freeze. The scenic canyon between Cheyenne Crossing and the town of Spearfish is one of the recommended attractions of the northern Black Hills. South Dakota Tourism

The Homestake Mining Company maintains an extensive rail system at the various levels of its operations more than a mile below the earth's surface. Electric locomotives have replaced horses and mules for towing the ore cars. Wall Drug Store collection

A century apart, two steam locomotives towed their trains along scenic Black Hills routes. One catered to tourists and railroad hobbyists of a later generation, opposite page, while the other toiled through Rapid Canyon on a work-a-day freight and passenger run. South Dakota Tourism, opposite page; South Dakota State Historical Society, next right

One of the worst tragedies in South Dakota history occurred on June 9 and 10, 1972, when 237 lives were lost in the Rapid City flood. An estimated 4.3 billion gallons of water poured through the city with little advance warning, causing some $160 million in damages and leaving freak reminders, like this automobile pile-up, in its destructive wake. U.S. Department of the Interior, Geological Survey

Flying high above Mount Rushmore was
an EC-135 airborne command post, one of
many different types of planes stationed at
Ellsworth Air Force Base through the
years. Initially established in 1942 as the
Rapid City Army Air Field for the training
of B-17 "Flying Fortress" crews, the
strategic installation was renamed in 1953
for Brigadier General Richard Ellsworth,
commander of the 28th Strategic Recon-
naissance Wing, who died in the crash of a
Rapid City-based RB-36 in Newfoundland
the same year. Ellsworth Air Force Base

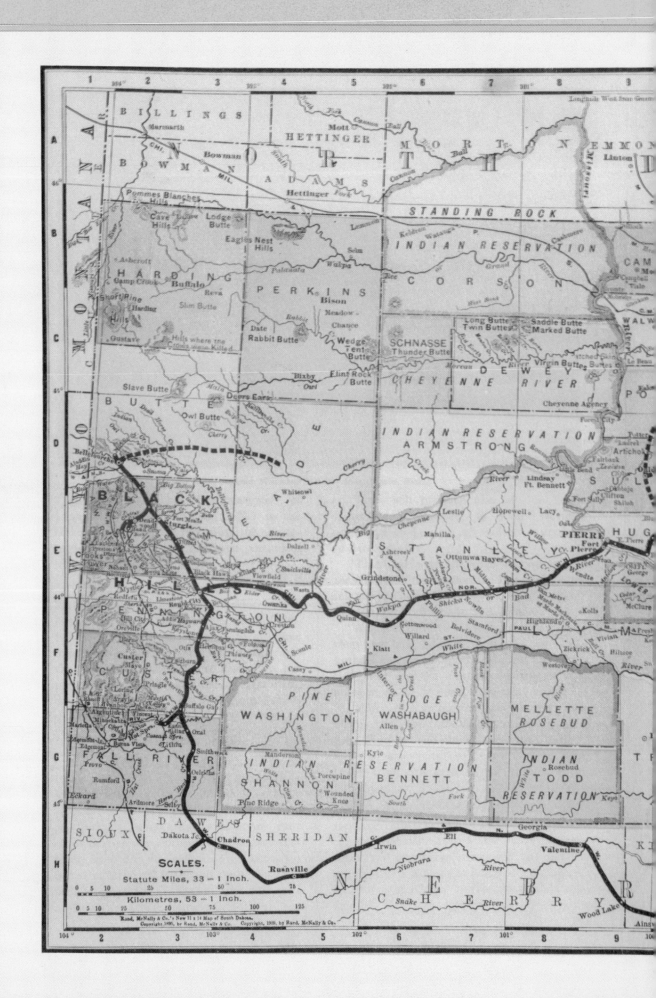

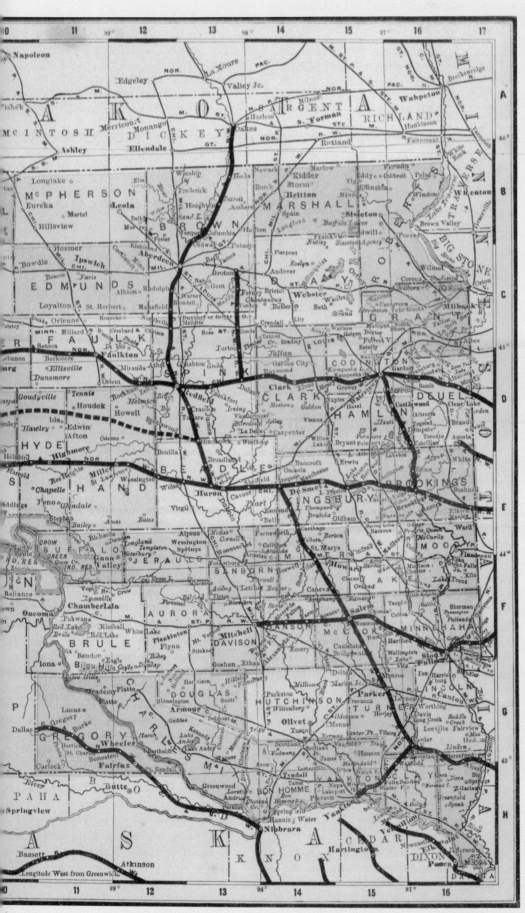

From a geographic standpoint, South Dakota is not totally unlike a half dozen or more Great Plains states. The Black Hills spill over into Wyoming and Montana, and North Dakota boasts the Badlands of the Little Missouri. The prairie lands begin in Canada and descend all the way to Texas. Minnesota may have 10,000 lakes, but it takes a lot of blue ink to print a South Dakota road map, too. East-river fields rival Iowa for corn yields, and Nebraska ranchers would be proud to run their calves on west-river grass.

What is it, then, that makes South Dakota unique? In part, it is that very diversity of the land. But even more, it is in the shared experiences of the people who live in the spacious, blue-skyed state.

Where else in the United States has a population decried for so many years the military massacre of a virtually defenseless band of Indians; established a splendid state capital in a small isolated town; tamed a wild river with four huge dams; welcomed two sculptors with mountain-size dreams; prayed routinely for rains to moisten parched ground; saved the buffalo from extinction and imported pheasants and salmon; built cities with dinosaur parks and corn palaces; and fashioned a governmental system that prides itself on a "pay as you go" philosophy?

People who have lived those experiences, or who have come later to inhabit a state with such a heritage, can be expected to exhibit some common characteristics. The blizzards and drouths and economic downturns of farming have caused Dakotans to be persistent to the point of dogged tenacity. Quests for gold in the hills and visions of prosperous farmsteads on the flatlands give clear evidence that these are a people eager for challenge.

Though there are always exceptions, for the most part South Dakotans will agree that they live where they do, not especially for the pursuit of wealth, but for a way of life that offers elbow room, good neighbors, oceanic sunrises and an everyday chance to commune with nature.

A 1909 map of South Dakota shows the importance of railroads to the state at that time. Watertown, Aberdeen and Sioux Falls had numerous lines spider-webbing out in all directions. Eliot S. Muxfelt collection

That very association with nature might also account for the quiet, steady optimism that exists, especially in the rural communities. One old-timer, waiting out still another dry spell, remarked to a radio interviewer: "You know, it always rains after a drouth." It was his way of saying that even the worst of problems have a way of working themselves out.

A half-century before South Dakota was admitted to the Union, Daniel Webster noted that "When tillage begins, other professions follow. The farmers, therefore, are the founders of civilization." Webster's wisdom was prophetically descriptive of the development of South Dakota. Once farms were established, the state's cities and towns became centers for the arts, commerce, education and the trades. Interestingly, the people who choose to move to the state in the late 20th century value the same qualities of life and do-it-yourself opportunities that brought the first pioneers 100 or more years earlier.

While South Dakota remains probably the most rural state in the nation, several of its cities have experienced dramatic growth because of tourism and industrial development. Most notable is Sioux Falls, where city planners have even had to fret over an occasional traffic jam. Still, no one can deny—or wants to—that South Dakota is principally a farm state. Bankers and lawyers are apt to talk crops and cattle with nearly as much ease as those men and women who actually raise them. Part of the reason for that is due to the importance of the farm dollar to the entire state's economy. Even urbane shops in the larger cities feel the pinch when the hog market sours.

Another reason is that many of the leading townspeople are farm boys or farm girls who grew up milking cows, walking beans and stacking hay. More than one South Dakota professional has looked out from an air-conditioned office on a sunshiney day in June, wishing for another opportunity to steer a John Deere down a corn row again.

Other states have lakes and mountains, plainsland and rivers. But nowhere else will you find a people quite like South Dakotans!

The traditional hat and boots are the identifying marks of South Dakota ranchers of all generations. South Dakota Tourism, Bill Goehring photo

True ranchers have learned to respect the fragile soil of the western prairie and its primary adaptability to cattle-raising. There were times when thousands of grassland acres were plowed up and seeded to wheat and other crops, and when dry years came, erosion was severe and disastrous. South Dakota Tourism

252

Mainstreet Vermillion blushes with Coyote Red every fall when University of South Dakota homecoming festivities kick off with the Dakota Day parade of cheerleaders, bands, floats and ever-present politicians. Law, medicine, business administration and communications are leading courses at the university, which boasts such noted graduates as television newsman Tom Brokaw, Joe Robbie, whose Miami Dolphins won Superbowl championships, and Allan H. Neuharth, chairman of the Gannett Corporation and founder of the national newspaper U.S.A. Today. South Dakota State University

McCrory Gardens in Brookings is often called "the prettiest 70 acres in South Dakota." Named for Sam McCrory, former head of the horticulture department at South Dakota State University, the colorful display is considered to be one of the top ten ornamental and research gardens in the United States. South Dakota Tourism

253

Milbank's most famous landmark through the years has been the wind-operated gristmill built incongruously by an Englishman named Henry Holland in 1886. One of the few of its kind in the United States, the relic of pioneer days has been restored and is a continuing tourist attraction. Otter Tail Power Company

Sioux Falls was settled beside the scenic cascades of the Big Sioux River. Indians called them minne waukon *(sacred water), but pioneer entrepreneurs saw the falls as a potential energy source for flour mills, power plants and other commercial enterprises. South Dakota Tourism, Paul Horsted photo*

The faces on Mount Rushmore are subject to periodic inspections for possible defects. Gutzon Borglum wanted his sculpture to last for thousands of years "until the wind and rain alone shall wear them down." Maintenance workers patch any cracks with a mixture of granite dust, white lead and linseed oil, a formula recommended by Borglum himself. South Dakota Tourism

Although early settlers of South Dakota represented many ethnic groups, the predominant pioneers were of Scandinavian descent. Norwegian immigrants were especially numerous, and a century after the Great Dakota Boom, Augustana College in Sioux Falls paid homage to that heritage by establishing the Nordland Fest, a celebration featuring Norwegian foods, crafts and cultures. South Dakota Tourism

State high school basketball tournaments reach almost World Series proportions in South Dakota. They are held in several major arenas like the Rapid City Civic Center, which also provides sophisticated facilities for such varied events as concerts, art shows and national conventions. South Dakota Tourism

Some kiddingly call it South Dakota's favorite winter sport: following the goings-on of the state legislature when lawmakers meet during the early months of each year in Pierre. While the elected representatives have traditionally been of a conservative nature, a streak of prairie populism is often evident, especially in matters pertaining to the family farm and the general agricultural economy. South Dakota Tourism

From a tranquil rural setting north of Sioux Falls, scientists at the Earth Resources Observation Systems (EROS) Data Center receive, process and distribute photographic images from the government's Landsat satellite sensors and from airborne mapping cameras. Part of the EROS mission is to provide earth-science information that will help ensure that public lands and resources are managed wisely for the people of today and tomorrow. EROS Data Center

This mosaic of South Dakota was pieced together from 15 Landsat satellite images acquired from nearly 600 miles above the earth. Green vegetation photographs in red. Note the heavy greenery of the Black Hills forests and its lack in the Badlands region. EROS Data Center

Taken almost a century apart, these two photos seem to show that the South Dakota farm scene has not changed much—except that single-cross corn seeds have been replaced by hybrid varieties, and chemical fertilizers, herbicides and pesticides, for better or for worse, have increased yields considerably. *South Dakota State Historical Society, Frank Cundill photo, left; Vermillion Plain Talk, Ron Johnson photo, below*

The rural mail carriers of Freeman switched from horses to Indian motorcycles in the early 1900s. They caused many heads to turn when they first putt-putted down the country roads of Hutchinson County. Pine Hill Printery

In both west-river and east-river country, the railroads played a leading role in the development of town and rural areas alike. There were a few mishaps, of course, but— barring floods and blizzards—schedules generally were maintained, and there was great dependence upon the regular comings and goings of freight and passenger trains. South Dakota State Historical Society

Growing up on a South Dakota homestead wasn't all bad—especially if you had a doll, a Dan Patch wagon, a baby sister and a fancy window awning to keep out the summer sun. South Dakota State Historical Society, Frank Cundill photo

These men posed with a toddy after serving as pallbearers at the funeral of W. H. Ball, who was a pioneer in Lincoln County after the Civil War. Their apparel indicated what a well-dressed South Dakotan was wearing early in the 20th century. Yankton County Historical Society

259

The innovative Peter Norbeck (standing), a former well-driller, was elected governor of South Dakota in 1916 and U.S. senator four years later. The progressive Republican was instrumental in creating Custer State Park, arranging financing for the Rushmore Memorial and designing the unusual pigtails of the scenic Iron Mountain Road. Though always popular with farmers, he was sometimes at odds with city conservatives becaue of his populist ideas, among them the controversial Rural Credits program, which eventually cost the state more than $50 million. South Dakota State Historical Society

Homesteading mothers had little time or opportunity for education, but by the late 1890s their daughters were attending college in increasing numbers. This turn-of-the-century photo was taken in the women's study room at South Dakota Agricultural College in Brookings. South Dakota State University

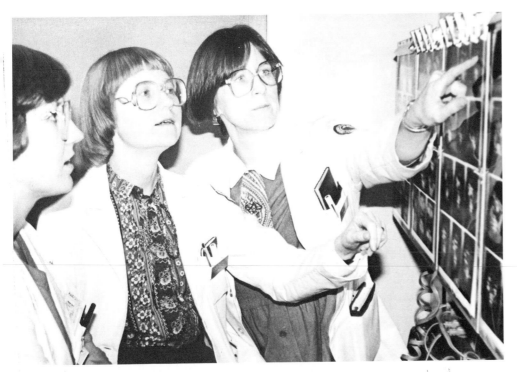

The University of South Dakota's four-year School of Medicine graduated its first class in 1978. Its purpose was to alleviate the shortage of physicians in the state's rural areas. An increasing number of women doctors was a welcome bonus from the "school without walls," which parceled students out to teaching hospitals and clinics throughout the state for many of their classes. *South Dakota State University*

In South Dakota, pigs have always been known as "mortgage lifters." Through the years, demand has changed from huge lard hogs of the early 1900s (above) to lean-meat animals bred for a more diet-conscious generation. *South Dakota State Historical Society, above; M. Jill Sundstrom photo, left*

The family garden was usually an added responsibility for Dakota homesteaders' wives. They then canned as much of the crop as they could or stored it in a root cellar, which often doubled as a refuge from storms. Timber Lake and Area Historical Society, Frank Cundill photo

Long before girls' basketball became a highly competitive sport in South Dakota high schools and colleges, young ladies of another era wore bloomers as they partici-pated in a less physical version of the game. This was the Sioux Falls Cathedral High School team of 1927. David W. Kemp collection

The De Smet News *took advantage of an Old Settlers Day parade to promote "Ladies' Calling Cards, 25 for 15 cents." The women accompanying the float were dressed in the finery of 1900. South Dakota Press Association*

When he wasn't tending his flower garden, Joseph Wiley rang a bell to warn of approaching trains at the Milbank station. It was unique, but not necessarily the busiest job in the state. Grant County Review collection

A Walt Disney movie titled "The Family Band" was based on the musical sons and daughters of Cal Bower and his wife. The exception was Alice (front row, left) who started her career as a typesetter for the Vermillion Standard *and later married Joe Gossage, publisher of the* Rapid City Journal. *She assumed editorial control of the paper when her husband became ill and became the first woman elected to the South Dakota Newspaper Hall of Fame. Emily Myers collection*

Tough, tenacious, independent, hard-working, neighborly but sometimes wary of strangers—the South Dakota homesteaders clung to the land through good times and bad. Many of their children and children's children succeeded them on farms that have remained in the same families for more than a century. South Dakota State Historical Society

The annual Freeman Schmeckfest, begun in 1959 to benefit the Freeman Junior College and Academy, features traditional German foods, including bratwurst and cheese pockets (varaniky), shown being prepared for the "festival of tasting." Because of the concentration of Mennonites in the area, Freeman was supposed to have been named Menno, but local lore has it that railroad workers mixed up the sign-boards and the neighboring town ended up with a name intended for the other. Freeman Courier, Tim Waltner photos

Arne Larson started to save musical instruments after 1920 when the U.S. Congress passed legislation that required new American instruments to drop a half step in pitch to fall in line with European standards. Good instruments became obsolete, and Arne, a musician and pack rat, acquired them. He went to Brookings as a music teacher in 1943 and continued to collect. By 1966, his large home was bursting with antique flugelhorns, unique violins and other unusual musical paraphernalia, and the University of South Dakota offered him a faculty position and a home for his collection. Today the Shrine to Music in Vermillion is a world-class museum visited by thousands. South Dakota Magazine

The soil of the James River valley is well suited to growing melons, squash and pumpkins. Forestburg in Sanborn County is the watermelon capital of the region, but throughout the valley the potential for fruit growing and truck gardening has gone virtually untapped since pioneer times. This lad found a pumpkin-seat and a tasty apple at Garrity's Prairie Gardens, a commercial orchard near Mission Hill. South Dakota Magazine

Alligator wrestling provides a summer job for collegians brave enough to work at Reptile Gardens near Rapid City. It is one of numerous commercial tourist attractions in the Black Hills, where tourism is a major industry. Black Hills, Badlands & Lakes Association

Annual turtle races in Volin (below) and mud-wrestling pigs at the Clay County Fair in Vermillion (left) proved that it didn't always take sophisticated activities to entertain small-town crowds in South Dakota. Missouri Valley Observer, *below;* Vermillion Plain Talk, *Tom Nelson photo, left*

South Dakota doesn't have any more two-gun cowboys, but two-pole fishermen are common along the state's streams and lakes. Fishing laws permit anglers to double their odds for catching a great variety of species, some with very high limits allowed. South Dakota Tourism, Jayne Erickson photo

4-H calves and errant bulls can be equally stubborn. A future farmer tugged at his show animal at the annual Watertown Farm Show (left), while it took a cowhand and the law to corral an obstinate Hereford that got loose in the same city. Watertown Public Opinion

South Dakota's black population has been relatively small through the years, although colonies of former slaves settled in the Onida and Yankton areas as early as the mid-1880s. In 1885, one of their number, A. L. Lewis, built the African Methodist Episcopal Church in Yankton. It was still being used a century later. South Dakota Magazine

A sense of humor is an important ingredient for survival on a family farm. Near Gayville in Yankton County a rural humorist caused passing motorists to stop and stare at a depiction of what can happen if one is careless around a hay baler. And near Vermillion a smiling barn added a bright note to the countryside. Missouri Valley Observer, *above;* Argus Leader, *Lloyd B. Cunningham photo, left*

South Dakota's many citizens of Norwegian descent have often borne the brunt of a special brand of humor. E. C. "Red" Stangland, a radio station owner, capitalized on the practice by issuing a series of Norske joke books, featuring Lena and Ole, lutefisk and lefse stories. *South Dakota Magazine*

The University of South Dakota's Dakota-Dome sports complex with an inflatable roof was an ideal spot for testing an inflatable Raggedy Ann balloon created by Raven Industries of Sioux Falls for the 1984 Macy's Thanksgiving Day Parade in New York City. The Dome gave the state badly needed indoor facilities for late fall and winter athletic contests and other events. *Vermillion Plain Talk, Ron Johnson photo*

Huge catfish—making up in size what they lack in pulchritude—still thrive in the Missouri and tributaries such as the Jim and the Big Sioux. According to local lore, the first Christmas dinner in Yankton in 1859 consisted primarily of catfish, boiled mush and molasses. M. Jill Sundstrom photo

They say you can take the boy out of the country but you can't take the country out of the boy. The same applies to youngsters from ranching country. Richard D. Hurd grew up in Meade County. When he became a circuit court judge in Sioux Falls, he donned the judicial black robe, but his boots proclaimed his west river roots. Argus Leader, *Mike Sierra photo*

South Dakotans—living in what is said to be the nation's most agricultural state—are especially close to nature and to animal life, both wild and domestic. A cuddly raccoon and an affectionate bovine typify that relationship. M. Jill Sundstrom photos

The coyote is the official state animal. It also lends its name to the athletic teams of the University of South Dakota. University of South Dakota

Gladys Pyle opened the door for women in South Dakota politics when she was elected to the state house of representatiaves in 1922. Four years later she became the first female constitutional officer, serving two terms as secretary of state. She broke still another barrier in 1938 when she won an election to a "short term" in the U.S. Senate following the death of Peter Norbeck. In her 90s she was still promoting another Republican candidate, Jim Abdnor, who defeated George McGovern in a senatorial race. South Dakota Magazine

South Dakota has the unique experience of having two native sons as back-to-back Democratic candidates for the presidency of the United States. George McGovern (at left), a college professor born in Avon, and Hubert H. Humphrey, a native of Wallace who had worked in the family drug store in Huron. Both were defeated by Richard M. Nixon. McGovern served as a United States senator and Humphrey was the nation's vice president under Lyndon B. Johnson. South Dakota State University

When South Dakota celebrated the 100th anniversary of the creation of Dakota Territory in 1961, the state's congressional delegation helped promote the centennial. They were (from left): Senator Karl E. Mundt, Representative E. Y. Berry, Representative Ben Reifel and Senator Francis Case. Reifel was the first Sioux Indian to attain such high political office. Because of its limited population, South Dakota lost one of its two congressmen in 1982. Karl E. Mundt Historical and Educational Foundation

Politically, South Dakota was long considered a rock-solid Republican state, but that changed after World War II. In 1974, Republican Larry Pressler, a former Rhodes Scholar from Humboldt, read of his upset victory over Frank Denholm for a seat in congress, while Democrats Richard Kneip and George McGovern were re-elected. At right, Pressler, then student body president at the University of South Dakota, gave up his trousers to Mike Raffety, his counterpart at South Dakota State University, after the Jackrabbits defeated the Coyotes 61-0 in the 1963 Hobo Day football game. Pressler later became a U.S. senator. Watertown Public Opinion, above; South Dakota State University Alumni Association, right

Railroad tracks once crisscrossed the state and literally provided its life blood. Little by little many of the lines were abandoned. A few became biking and hiking trails, others were reclaimed by nature after the rails were pulled up and sold for scrap. Missouri Valley Observer, *Bernie Hunhoff photo*

This book would not have been possible without the complete cooperation of the board of directors of the South Dakota State Historical Society, which generously approved the use of its extensive photographic collection as the nucleus of this pictorial sampler. Other institutions under its direction—the Robinson Museum in Pierre, the W. H. Over Museum in Vermillion and the Agricultural Heritage Museum in Brookings—also shared their resources.

Similarly, the board of directors of the South Dakota Art Museum in Brookings made available reproductions of the works of artist Harvey Dunn which, in themselves, tell a story of the state's pioneering days.

Special thanks go to Dr. Thomas Kilian for originally involving the authors in this "labor of love" project; to Bonnie Gardner, zealous guardian of pictures for the State Historical Society; and to Myrna Hunhoff and Phyllis Karolevitz "for many things."

The South Dakota Department of Tourism—and especially talented photographers Paul Horsted and Mark Kayser—were extremely helpful, as were Donald J. Binder, curator of the Yankton County Historical Society Museum; Joel Strasser, an artist with a camera; Ted Hustead of the Wall Drug Store; and Clyde Goin, whose personal collection added immeasurably to the final product.

Other individuals and organizations deserving gratitude for various reasons include Robert E. Kolbe, Jim Nelson and the Timber Lake and Area Historical Society, the Center for Western Studies, David W. Kemp, Sharon Wiese and the Douglas County Historical Society, the Sioux Falls *Argus Leader*, Bob Lee, EROS Data Center, Joseph Stewart, Phyllis Justice and the *Grant County Review*, Elliot S. Muxfelt, Tom Nelson and the Vermillion *Plain Talk*, the Mitchell Corn Palace, Codington County Historical Society, Buechel Memorial Lakota Museum at St. Francis Indian Mission, Glenn Gering, South Dakota National Guard Museum, St. Joseph's Indian School, Hubert E. Alewel and the *Chamberlain Register*.

Siouxland Heritage Museum, Karl E. Mundt Historical and Educational Foundation, *Watertown Public Opinion*, Father Stanislaus Maudlin and Blue Cloud Abbey, South Dakota State University, the *Missouri Valley Observer*, Friends of the Middle Border Museum, Bert Moritz and the *Clark County Courier*, John Day and the Oscar Howe family, the University of South Dakota, Richard V. Johnson, Tim Waltner and the *Freeman Courier*, Winifred Reutter, William Lampe and the Dakotaland Museum, Keith M. Jensen and the South Dakota Press Association, M. Jill Sundstrom, Bonnie Kempel of Norwest Banks, Chad Kono of the South Dakota State University Alumni Association, Larry Atkinson and Jo Hall of the *Mobridge Tribune*, Gene Hexom of East River Electric, Ellsworth Air Force Base, Al Kubosek of the Otter Tail Power Company and the Black Hills, Badlands & Lakes Association.

To any others who aided and abetted this endeavor and have been inadvertently overlooked, the authors both apologize and express a heartfelt thanks to you in your anonymity.

After a century of statehood, South Dakota's heritage has been amply preserved by authors, historians, journalists, artists and photographers. Moreover, this treasury of pen, brush and lens is being continually enriched by local histories, biographies, pictorial collections and other memorabilia of a pioneer past. The bibliography that follows is a mere sampling of the scores of books available on the whole or the various parts of the South Dakota story. Not included, but of inestimable value, are the many volumes of the *South Dakota Historical Collection* dating back to 1902 and the quarterly editions of *South Dakota History,* both publications of the South Dakota State Historical Society. Newspaper microfilms, personal diaries, student theses, scrapbooks and the papers presented annually at history conferences all add to the literature of the Land of Infinite Variety, assuring that yesterday will be well-remembered today and tomorrow.

Armstrong, Moses K. *The Early Empire Builders of the Great West.* St. Paul: E. W. Porter, 1901.

Blasingame, Ike. *Dakota Cowboy: My Life in the Old Days.* New York: G. P. Putnam's Sons, 1958.

Casey, Robert J. *The Black Hills and Their Incredible Characters.* Indianapolis: The Bobbs-Merrill Company, Inc., 1949.

Chittenden, Hiram M. *History of Early Steamboat Navigation on the Missouri River.* New York: Francis P. Harper, 1903.

Clowser, Don C. *Dakota Indian Treaties.* Deadwood, South Dakota: privately printed, 1974.

Coursey, Oscar W. *Who's Who in South Dakota* (5 vols.). Mitchell, South Dakota: Educator Supply Company, 1916.

Dick, Everett. *The Sod-House Frontier, 1854-1890.* Lincoln, Nebraska: Johnsen Publishing Company, 1954.

Eastman, Charles A. *From the Deep Woods to Civilization.* Boston: Little, Brown and Company, 1916.

Fielder, Mildred. *Railroads of the Black Hills.* Seattle: Superior Publishing Company, 1964.

____. *The Treasure of Homestake Gold.* Aberdeen, South Dakota: North Plains Press, 1970.

Fite, Gilbert C. *Mount Rushmore.* Norman, Oklahoma: University of Oklahoma Press, 1952.

Hanson, Joseph Mills. *The Conquest of the Missouri.* Chicago: A. C. McClurg & Co., 1909.

Hart, Wesley R. and Lass, William E. *Frontier Photographer: Stanley J. Morrow's Dakota Years.* Lincoln, Nebraska: University of Nebraska Press, 1956.

Karolevitz, Robert F. *Challenge: The South Dakota Story.* Sioux Falls, South Dakota: Brevet Press, Inc., 1975.

____. *Where Your Heart Is: The Story of Harvey Dunn, Artist.* Aberdeen, South Dakota: North Plains Press, 1970.

____. *With a Shirt Tail Full of Type: The Story of Newspapering in South Dakota.* Freeman, South Dakota: South Dakota Press Association, 1982.

____. *Yankton: A Pioneer Past.* Aberdeen, South Dakota: North Plains Press, 1972.

Kingsbury, George W. *History of Dakota Territory* (5 vols.). Chicago: The S. J. Clarke Publishing Company, 1915.

Krause, Herbert and Olson, Gary D. *Custer's Prelude to Glory.* Sioux Falls, South Dakota: Brevet Press, Inc., 1974.

Lamar, Howard Roberts. *Dakota Territory, 1861-1889: A Study of Frontier Politics.* New Haven, Connecticut: Yale University Press, 1956.

Lee, Bob and Williams, Dick. *Last Grass Frontier.* Sturgis, South Dakota: Black Hills Publishers, Inc., 1964.

Milton, John R. *South Dakota.* New York: W. W. Norton Publishing Company, 1977.

Nelson, Bruce. *Land of the Dakotahs.* Minneapolis: University of Minnesota Press, 1946.

Nelson, Paula M. *After the West Was Won: Homesteaders and Town-Builders in Western South Dakota, 1900-1917.* Iowa City: University of Iowa Press, 1986.

Oyos, Lynwood E., ed. *Over a Century of Leadership: South Dakota Territorial and State Governors.* Sioux Falls, South Dakota: Center for Western Studies, 1987.

Parker, Watson. *Gold in the Black Hills.* Norman, Oklahoma: University of Oklahoma Press, 1966.

Pressler, Larry. *U.S. Senators from the Prairie.* Vermillion, South Dakota: Dakota Press, 1982.

Rezatto, Helen. *Tales of the Black Hills.* Aberdeen, South Dakota: North Plains Press, 1983.

Robinson, Doane. *History of South Dakota* (2 vols.). Chicago: B. F. Bowen and Company, 1904.

____. *History of South Dakota* (3 vols.). Chicago: The American Historical Society, Inc., 1930.

Rølvaag, O. E. *Giants in the Earth.* New York: Harper and Bros., 1924.

Schell, Herbert S. *A History of South Dakota.* Lincoln, Nebraska: University of Nebraska Press, 1961.

Schuler, Harold H. *The South Dakota Capitol in Pierre.* Pierre, South Dakota: State Publishing Company, 1985.

South Dakota Guide. Federal Writers' Project, Works Progress Administration. Pierre, South Dakota: State Publishing Company, 1938.

South Dakota Place Names. South Dakota Writers' Project, Works Progress Administration. Vermillion, South Dakota: University of South Dakota, 1941.

Zeitner, June Culp and Borglum, Lincoln. *Borglum's Unfinished Dream: Mount Rushmore.* Aberdeen, South Dakota: North Plains Press, 1976

Bob Karolevitz and Bernie Hunhoff can offer a two-generation view of their native state.

They were both born in Yankton's Sacred Heart Hospital, 29 years apart. They are each graduates of Yankton High School, 29 years apart. Their college degrees are similar: Bob majored in printing and rural journalism at South Dakota State College (now University), and Bernie earned his sheepskin in communications media at Mount Marty College.

Similarities continued in their respective careers. They each had early newspaper experience, and both wrote promotional material for U.S. congressmen: Bob for Thor Tollefson of Washington and Bernie for Frank Denholm of South Dakota. Each then moved on to other public relations work before opting to strike out on their own.

In 1978, Hunhoff started the weekly *Observer* in his basement in Gayville, South Dakota. It developed into an award-winning newspaper, which he eventually sold. In 1985 he began publishing *South Dakota Magazine* which, like the *Observer,* quickly gained wide acceptance.

Karolevitz, who took time out for military service in World War II and Korea, has been a freelance writer for more than three decades, having more than two dozen books to his credit, as well as hundreds of articles and features.

Though of disparate ages, the two began working together when Bernie asked Bob if he would write a column for the *Observer.* Bob said yes, and later agreed to produce a regular piece for *South Dakota Magazine.* The newspaper columns were collected in two popular books: *Tears in My Horseradish* and *Toulouse the Goose and Other Ridiculous Stories.* Both volumes were brightened by Bernie's fun photography.

Bob and Bernie each married native South Dakotans in Yankton. Phyllis has been Bob's working partner in his writing ventures and in Dakota Homestead Publishers, which they own. Myrna has played a similar role in Bernie's publication enterprises. Both couples have two children, and both live on Yankton County farms to which they escape from their typewriter commitments.

Needless to say, it is somehow appropriate that with their uniquely paralleling careers they should collaborate on this pictorial sampler of their mutually favorite state, *Uniquely South Dakota!*

287